MW00511816

Success
Through Spirituality
For Women
BY BARBARA GRAY

Success
Through Spirituality
For Women

BARBARA GRAY PROACTIVES
399 Old Canton Road
Marietta, Georgia 30068
404-971-0179

Copyright 1995 by Barbara Gray
Cover design by Bill Wyatt

ISBN 0-9637784-4-7

Printed in the United States

Contents

Dedication

My original goal in 1995 was to spend the year marketing my books, *Life's Instruction Books for Women,* on radio and television and doing book signings. However, several women I met asked me how to start a business and take responsibility for their lives. The Holy Spirit led me to follow a better plan and teach that which I had learned. So I dedicate this book to all women as they search for meaning and purpose in their lives by revealing their true selves.

Love,

Barbara

Risk

To laugh is to risk appearing the fool.
To weep is to risk appearing sentimental.
To reach for another is to risk involvement.
To expose your feelings is to risk exposing your
true self.
To place your ideas, your dreams before a crowd
is to risk their loss.
To love is to risk not being loved in return.
To live is to risk dying.
To believe is to risk despair.
To try is to risk failure.
But risks must be taken, because the greatest hazard
in life is to risk nothing.
The person who risks nothing, does nothing, has
nothing, is nothing.
They may avoid suffering and sorrow, but they
cannot learn, feel, change, grow, love, live.
Chained by their attitudes they are slaves; they have
forfeited their freedom.
Only a person who risks is free.

Written by an anonymous Chicago Teacher

(Hopefully Not Your Usually Boring)

Introduction

The successful life depends on taking responsibility- being proactive in your life. ◆ *YOU* ◆ *make the decision that YOU will be responsible.*

Your Life	You have given the responsiblity to?	Who should take the responsbility for your SUCCESS?
spirituality		
happiness		
finances		
growth	Parents?	YOU
relationships	Friends?	YOU
purpose	Husband?	YOU
integrity	Lover?	YOU
physical body	Children?	YOU
mentality	Bosses?	YOU
	Others?	YOU

If you did not find yourself in all the areas of column three, you at least know where you need to begin.

Doing the research and my own inner thinking for this book has taught me several truths that I hope you will also learn. First, no matter what the time or circumstance, strong successful women throughout history have taken responsibility and serviced the lives of others. They have chosen to do the right thing no matter the price or hardship.

I

First You Must:

✓ Seek your purpose in life which gives you all meaning and directions

✓ You must recognize that the focus of your purpose changes as you live the stages of your life.

✓ When you take responsibility for achieving your purpose you will be aligning with the flow of your life.

✓ You will live a life that is directed, purposeful, non-judgemental of self and others, willing to change, grow, and become all it can be.

✓ Understanding, awareness, creativity, and thinking will direct your actions rather than emotions and reactions to others and events.

You will know the best solutions, answers, words, actions, and thoughts to deal with whatever happens in your life.

God has provided everything within us to be everything we are to be. We are only to remove the layers of self-doubt, fear, self-hate, and criticism to reveal His Magnificent creation.

Choose FREEDOM! Free the true you by taking time to know yourself: your strengths, your weaknesses, your qualities, your soul, your spirit, your energy, your essence, your being.

And here we are in the 1990's with all the advantages and opportunities placed on a tray before us and many still refuse to take the action and responsibility for having a successful and fulfilled life.

STRONG WOMEN are opposing large corporations and saying I won't buy your products or work for you... if your attitude and advertising are demeaning to women, you have unfair pay scales and unequal opportunities, you turn your head to sexual harassment or your products are not ecologically sound.

STRONG WOMEN are taking responsibility for their health and safety by learning about their bodies and taking responsibility for what goes in them and happens to them.

STRONG WOMEN are willing to make:
changes
sacrifices
commitments
their own choices
deliberate moves in the right direction

Successful living has an orderliness of events which has to take place.

Strong Role Models Throughout History

You've Come a Long Way
But Don't Call You Baby!

The following history is selected obstacles, successes, and roles women have played. In studying our heritage, I think we not only need to thank the great women who came before us and made it possible to do the things we are doing today, but we need to look at ourselves and see if we are battling the prejudices, injustices, and stupidity as strongly as our predecessors. What responsibility do you feel toward the freedom of women to fulfill their potential?

"When you talk to young girls these days about their role models, very few mention a chemist like Madame Curie, or an astrophysicist and astronaut like Sally Ride, or a zoologist like Jane Goodall. Instead, they look to someone like Madonna, whose inspiring achievement in life is to parade around in her underwear while proclaiming herself to be a "material girl." *And people wonder why the country's in trouble.*"

Wynetka Ann Reynolds

Success Through Spirituality For Women

Studying the history of women, really for the first time, has been most revealing and interesting. Probably only a small percentage of women know much about the women who preceded them and their lives. When I went to college there were no women's studies, and one had to pick up random information and to admire the strong women who made history.

We owe it to ourselves to study the books coming out now about the history of women. We have made great achievements but we were not recognized for them. For too long most of us have not chosen to make new history and were still accepting the former attitudes and positions that were passed down. **"We must remember that one determined person can make a significant difference, and that a small group of determined people can change the course of history."** Sonia Johnson   I encourage you to read about the achievements of women as doctors and nurses, lawyers, actresses, writers, teachers, reformers, athletes, and performers to appreciate the obstacles they had to overcome and how they made it easier for us to fulfill our life's purpose. More importantly, I ask you to question what happened to our equality?

If women were acting as judges in Egypt and Sparta as the Bible verifies, what happened to our status when **Sandra Day O' Conner** can't find a law firm in the 1950's who is willing to hire a female. Because we were denied formal education and entrances to law school, we were denied legal protection through women lawyers and judges who would rule that women had rights to own property, were not the property of their fathers and husband, could attend schools of their choices, should receive equal pay, and had power over oppressors who tried to control them sexually, emotionally and mentally.

2

Strong Role Models Throughout History

We should question why the United States has never had a woman president when women have been rulers throughout history. Women such as **Hatshepsut** (1503-1482 B.C.) who ruled Egypt for 21 years and was one of the most powerful women of the Bronze Age. **Athaliah**, daughter of the famed Jezebel was born in 837 B.C. and became queen of Judah for seven years. As far back as 1750 B.C. the Middle Assyrian empire required that daughters, wives, widows, concubines, and sacred prostitutes had to wear veils. Common prostitutes had to leave their heads uncovered.

During the Middle Ages women lost a lot of the freedom and respect they had in earlier times as a result of the spread of Christianity and the philosophy of the Roman Catholic Church. Women were denied formal education.

There are now 50,000 women who serve as ministers and 400 women rabbis. Seminary classes are now 31% female. I enjoy attending a church with a female pastor because her talks are always uplifting and informative. Unbelievably, there is some pay discrimination in this field.

While wars have killed women's sons and husbands, they have usually improved their lives because while the men were fighting, women took their positions at home running businesses, making armaments, and running the homes. For Example, after the Japanese invaded China prior to World War II women gained better rights. American women proved to be capable of filling men's positions during World War II. Their mistake was that they did not look ahead to the men's returning home and did not begin their own companies or have jobs that could not be taken away.

3

Success Through Spirituality For Women

In 1876 the British passed a law which said women, children, criminals, and "idiots" were not classed as persons. **Emily Ferguson Murphy**, who was appointed the first magistrate in the British Empire, challenged the law. Her position was upheld and the case started a re-evaluation of women's legal status throughout the British Empire.

Great women during the early 1900's started unions to get better working conditions and fewer working hours for women and children. In 1909 the International Ladies Garment Workers Union organized a successful strike by **20,000** New York City shirtwaist makers. These women were not messing around- 3,000 Jewish-American and Italian-American workers pledged, *"If I turn traitor to the cause I now pledge, may this hand wither from the arm I now raise!"*

And yet we read a magazine article today where workers at a bakery get kidney infections because they are not provided with adequate breaks or bathroom facilities. The hugely increased reported cases of sexual harassment tell us that the pervading attitude toward women hasn't changed. But we don't have to tolerate being treated as sex objects, second class citizens in our homes, church, schools, employment. We have the resources and power, thanks to the strong women who preceded us.

Until the 1930's, large families were the norm and women often worked outside of the home all day and then cooked, washed, and cleaned for their families. **Margaret Sanger,** a nurse, promoted the idea of birth control and was forced to leave the country fearing arrest. She formed the group called Planned Parenthood Federation of America. Yet with all the progress in birth control and sex education, unwed teenagers are having record numbers of unplanned children.

4

Strong Role Models Throughout History

What so many young women today do not realize is that education is what insures women's political, social, and economic rights. It gives them their power. Instead of focusing on developing their minds, they are dealing with the trivia and non thinking aspects of their lives. Women such as **Maria Louise Baldwin,** who became the first African-American woman to become a principal in Massachusetts, exemplified a stately, dignified woman who demonstrated through her life the benefits of learning and wisdom. Her forceful personality deeply impressed students and their parents, and the leading social and intellectual figures of the community. She was active in several organizations of African-American women She lectured across the country. She is a far cry from the uneducated whiners who tell their victim stories on television.

In 1987 **Johnnetta Cole** became the seventh president and the first African-American woman president of Spelman College, the oldest African-American women's college in the U.S. Describing herself as the first Spelman president with an explicitly feminist vision, she expressed a commitment to making the school a center for scholarship about African-American women. She calls herself **Sister President**, and has become known as a strong advocate for the liberal arts curriculum.

Women reformers would not have tolerated the mousy behavior some women exemplify today. It is often said that the hardships we endure as children make us stronger adults. **Carry Amelia Moore Nation** suffered poverty, a brother with mental instability, ill health, and an alcoholic husband who died leaving her with a child. She took a hatchet to saloons who were breaking prohibition laws. Her second husband divorced her in 1901 for desertion. She was arrested for disturbing the

5

peace, so she paid her fines from lecture fees and contributions and by selling souvenir hatchets. Numerous physical assaults because of her stance may have contributed to her ill health.

Fannie Lou Townsend Hamer is another strong lady who overcame early hardships to help gain rights and equality for others. The youngest of twenty children, she was working the fields with her parents by age six. The poverty and racial tensions which surrounded her only allowed her to receive a sixth-grade education. However, she joined the Student Nonviolent Coordinating Committee (SNCC), where she soon became a field secretary. She ran as a Mississippi Freedom Democratic Party (MFDP) candidate for Congress, and gave a nationally televised address describing the violence and injustices suffered by civil rights activists. She had personally suffered a beating in a jail which left her crippled. She continued campaigning actively and was awarded honorary degrees from several universities.

Maria Weston Chapman was a brave woman who exemplified being a risk taker through efforts to further her cause. In 1832 she helped organize the Boston Female Anti-Slavery Society. When Garrison was mobbed while attempting to address the society in October 1835, the meeting adjourned in stately procession to Chapman's home. In May 1838 she addressed the Anti-Slavery Convention of American Women in Philadelphia in defiance of a threatening mob. (The mob returned the next day and burned down the hall.). She was elected to the executive committee of the American Anti-Slavery Society. She assisted Garrison in establishing the National Anti-Slavery Standard in 1840.

So you think your tough beginning is an excuse not to succeed? Born in Chester, Pennsylvania, **Ethel**

Strong Role Models Throughout History

Waters grew up in extreme poverty, married before she was thirteen, and later worked as a chambermaid and scrubwoman. Encouraged by friends she started singing and went on to perform on the stage, in nightclubs, and in the movies. All black casts were making notable and uplifting movies during the 30's, not like many of the negative roles blacks play today. Waters won awards for outstanding movies. She wrote a best selling autobiography called *His Eye is on the Sparrow* and later appeared frequently with Billy Grahan in his crusades.

Born March 29, 1918, in Newport News, Virginia, **Pearl Mae Bailey** attended her father's church, the House of Prayer, a Holy Roller style congregation, where her love of dance, song and rhythm grew. Her performance in the title role of an all-black production of the musical Hello, Dolly! brought New York theater audiences to their feet nightly and won her a special Tony award; she was also named Entertainer of the Year by Cue Magazine.

In 1975 she was appointed special ambassador to the UN by Gerald Ford. She later enrolled at Georgetown and, at age 67, graduated with a bachelor's degree in theology. In 1988 Bailey received the Presidential Medal of Freedom from Ronald Reagan.

Mary Lou WIlliams, abandoned by her father when she was still a baby, but supported by a mother who did housework for others, went on to become a famous jazz pianist. Later known as the First Lady of Jazz and the Queen of Jazz, and as the first black to perform at Carnegie Hall, she began playing the piano at two. She founded Mary Records and the Bel Canto Foundation, a group dedicated to assisting artists and musicians with medical, drug, and alcohol problems. She was awarded the Guggenheim Fellowship twice, and many honorary doctorates. President Jimmy Carter asked her to perform at the White House.

Did you know that during the 1800's the violin was considered too much of a masculine instrument for women? Despite this, **Camilla Urso** started taking lessons at age six and a year later her parents took her to study at the Paris Conservatoire. She lived in the United States and traveled doing concerts throughout the world. A preeminent violinist of the day she was adept in classic and contemporary works.

Like a lot of other black musicians, **Sarah Vaughan** began her musical career in her church. At age 7 she was studying piano and organ and singing. She won an amateur contest at Harlem's Apollo Theater and went on to sing with Billy Eckstine, Dizzy Gillespie and Charlie Parker. Though she performed in the finest places in New York, audiences in southern cities did not want to hear her despite her ability as a contralto with a range of three octaves, earning the nickname *"The Divine One,"* and later being inducted into the Jazz Hall of Fame. She appeared in three movies and several Jazz Festivals.

We find women in the 90's who are afraid to drive on the interstate, travel from city to city by airplane, and make any kind of change in their unhappy lives. Predecessors like **Alla Nazimova** born in Russia, entered the dramatic school of the Philharmonic Society of Moscow at the age of seventeen. She came to New York after several successful performances in Europe. Nazimova was described as an actress of great intensity and powerful characterization. She went on playing roles in Hollywood of passionate and exotic women. She later performed on Broadway. She is known for performing with depth and intelligence and had a great command of her body, voice and expression and is

8

remembered as one of the most influential actresses of the American stage.

When Hollywood began to make movies **Lois Weber** (1881-1931) wrote scenarios, subtitles, acted, directed, designed sets and costumes, edited, and even developed negatives. She was described as energetic, aesthetically ambitious and technically well grounded. She wrote, produced and directed several successful films that dealt with relationships.

Thank goodness for the role and the importance of the **Virgin Mary.** She has always been extolled, worshipped, and accredited for numerous miracles. Women's interest in spirituality have always made them active in the churches and their beliefs have sustained them in their hardships. Women have always had important roles in religions but rarely have they lead the religion.

Dorothy Day helped found the Catholic Worker, a monthly newspaper, to carry the idea based on communal farming and the establishment of houses of hospitality for the urban poor. The Catholic Worker was an organ for pacifism and for the support of Catholic conscientious objectors during World War II. Later, Day was against nuclear weaponry and preparations for nuclear war. She took part in demonstrations for civil rights, against the Vietnam War, and in support of farm workers organizing in California. Day lived in the New York City house or at the Catholic Worker's farm in Tivoli, New York, in voluntary poverty.

My grandmother raised five daughters and a son in the hills of Eastern Kentucky. Aunt Hazel related the story of how my aunt Julia was beaten up once by her husband. She and Hazel went to my grandfather and told him Julia had a rat in her house and she needed to borrow a gun. The next time her husband threatened her, Julia brought out the gun from under her pillow and said she would blow off the head of the rat. She was never hit again.

Annie Oakley *became so good with firearms as a child and she hunted with such success that she was able to pay off the mortgage on the family farm.* She beat a vaudeville marksman named Frank Butler at a shooting match at 15. She married him and worked the Buffalo Bill Cody Wild West Show for 16 years. She could split a playing card held edge-on at 30 paces, shoot cigarettes from her husband's lips, and fill a playing card thrown in the air with holes. A train wreck left her partially paralyzed, but she recovered and returned to the stage.

Elizabeth Van Lew was against slavery so much that she influenced her family to free the domestic servants. She brought back information to the federal authorities when she brought Union prisoners food and clothing. She was able to gather important information from former servants. Crazy Bet, as she was called by the people of Richmond, was to send out coded messages to the Union. Bravely, she lived the rest of her life in Richmond despite being a social outcast. She protested her taxes because she was denied the vote.

Elizabeth Zane was a gutsy lady who volunteered to fetch powder at her brother's house located outside the fort. The Indian attackers, amazed and amused, shouted "squaw, squaw" and did not fire at first. When they realized what she was doing they shot, but only her clothing was pierced.

Nancy Ward, a Native American leader whose mother was Cherokee and father a Delaware **took her husband's place in battle when he died.** This earned her the name Beloved Woman and she became the leader of the woman's council. Twice she warned the settlers and soldiers of impending Cherokee attacks. Known as the Pochahontas of the West, numerous legends and tales were written about her.

Ann Hennis came to America, probably as an indentured servant, in 1761. When her husband was killed in battle she **dressed as a male, used a rifle and tomahawk, and became a frontier scout, messenger, spy, and Indian fighter.** She became widely known as the white squaw of the Kanawha and as Mad Ann. During an attack on Fort Lee by Native Americans she volunteered to ride a hundred miles to Fort Union, and returned on the third day with powder.

Study women's history and you will learn that women have always been power rulers and queens. **Eleanor of Aquitaine**, queen of France and queen of England, was not only wife to Louis VII, **she also fought next to him during the Second Crusade.** She headed a retinue which included several hundred women soldiers and nurses. She also ruled England as regent while her son, Richard I, was fighting in the Crusades. She was known as the queen mother of England in a public career that spanned 65 years. **She is recognized as one of the most powerful and astute women of her age.**

A story in the Bible tells how a father threw out his virgin daughter to appease attackers. Women have endured being considered a man's property and they have been refused ownership of property throughout history.

Fortunately some women stood up for our rights. After her divorce in 1906 **Hortense Sparks Malsch** studied law by correspondence and then worked as a county court reporter. She remarried and completed her legal studies. She received national publicity in the *Delineator magazine* when she urged a need for a married woman's property law in Texas. Because she lobbied vigorously, the Hortense Ward Law was enacted. She was also successful in working for a workmen's compensation system a 54-hour work week for employed women and a bill giving women the right to vote in primaries.

Women have always flourished in writing. **Sappho** was a Greek poet who was born in 610 B.C. Some of her work still survives. **Theano** was a Greek philosopher, mathematician and physician and also a writer who lived about the same time. **Diotima of Mantinea** was a Greek philosopher, priestess and teacher to Socrates. We need to study the regression of respect for women's mental abilities as time progressed. How could we have ended up in the 20th century with women in Mid East countries still enduring genital mutilation and women in so called progressive countries still enduring mental mutilation because ancient thoughts about their self worth are still being dictated.

Phillis Wheatley was brought over as a slave from Africa and taught English and later Greek and Latin by her owner Mrs. Wheatley and her daughters. Boston scholars were amazed when she translated a tale from Ovid. Her first book of poetry was published at the age of thirteen.

Later she was set free and she went on to marry an intelligent but irresponsible man named John Peters who eventually abandoned her. *Memoir and Poems of Phillis Wheatley, and Letters of Phillis Wheatley* were published after her death. Abolitionists often cited her work in order to show that there is no basis for believing in the innate intellectual inferiority among African Americans. They also stood up for the equal educational rights of blacks.

At times tragedies turn out to be blessings. **Alice Walker,** author of *The Color Purple* which won a Pulitzer Prize and was made into a Steven Spielberg movie, was one of eight children of Georgia share-croppers. She was blinded in one eye as a child so her mother gave her a typewriter and allowed her to write instead of doing chores. She graduated class valedictorian and graduated from Sarah Lawrence College. She wrote about sexist violence, civil rights, rape, pornography and difficult relationships.

Despite having to get her education from her brother's tutors, **Mercy Warren** who was born in 1728 went on to become a poet and historian of the American Revolution. She believed that women did not have inferior intellect but inferior opportunities.

It is no secret to most of us that when women work outside the home, they have the additional responsibility of the housework. Studies show that few men in the 20th century are doing their part. Wives should learn from the examples of women reformers.

Agnes Nestor was a frail woman who proved to be an articulate and strong leader of a strike against the glove factory where she worked in 1898. The company met all their demands and paid the workers back for the rent they were for forced to pay to fix the machines they used! Nestor spent her whole life establishing other unions, and fighting to cut work time from ten hours to eight hours. She worked for child-labor, minimum wage, maternity health, and woman-suffrage legislation.

We have fared better in sports than in some areas of our lives. Major disparities in school funding and pay for professional athletes has always existed. Several women have distinguished themselves as athletes.

In 1886 the first modern Olympics were held in Athens. Women were allowed to compete in the next games held in 1900. At the Stockholm Olympics in 1912 there was only one women's swimming event. **Fanny**

Success Through Spirituality For Women

Durack, an Australian swimmer won the women's 100-meter freestyle event, setting the first of her nine world records. She belonged to the Ladies Amateur Swimming Association of New South Wales which prohibited women from swimming in the presence of men.

As of the last Olympics, **Jackie Joyner-Kersee** has earned three gold medals, a silver and a bronze. She holds the American records in both the indoor and the outdoor long jump, as well as the world record in the heptathalon. Many describe her as the greatest living female athlete.

Florence Giffith Joyner is described as the "World's Fastest Woman." She has world records in the 100 and 200 meters. In 1988 she won three gold medals and one silver, a record for an American woman. Joyner attributes her success to *" I pray hard, work hard and leave the rest to God."*

Most Americans could list several famous male golf professionals, but how many know the name **Kathryne Whitworth**? Here's her successes: Leading money winner on the Ladies Professsional Golf Association tour from 1965-1973, the PGA player of the year seven times, and the Associated Press woman athlete of the year in '65 and '66. *In 1969 she passed Mickey Wright to become the leading all-time money winner on the tour and by 1981 she was the first woman golfer to pass the million-dollar mark.* She won every major tournament on the tour except for the U.S. Open. She was inducted into the LPGA Hall of Fame, the world Golf Hall of Fame and the Texas Sports Hall of Fame, and the International Women's Sports Hall of Fame.

Named the queen mother of American tennis, **Hazel Hotchkill** won her last title at the age of 68! She won the national amateur women's singles championship four times. She won doubles at the Wightman

14

tournament, and at Wimbledon. She was six times the U.S. doubles co-champion and 42 national titles.

Most of us know the accomplishments of **Marie Curie,** but women have always had abilities and interests in the sciences. Young women are being encouraged in the schools today to rediscover these areas.

Mary Watson Whitney's interest in astronomy began when she traveled to Burlington, Iowa to observe a solar eclipse in 1869. She graduated with a Masters from Vassar and studied mathematics and celestial mechanics at the University of Zurich. *She wanted to demonstrate that women could work as well as men in the sciences and began a program of research at Vassar, concentrating on double stars, variable stars, asteroids, comets, and the precise measurement of photographic plates.*

Women have gone through highs and lows in medicine. **Peneshet,** who lived in Egypt around 1500 was named director of physicians, and many other women were also physicians, embalmers, or worked preparing drugs. Women who used plants for natural healing were considered witches and burned at the stake. Now we are returning to plants as natural healers.

Mary Edwards Walker overcame the hardships of being a female doctor in the late 1800's was **the only female surgeon during the Civil War even wearing a modified Union uniform. She was imprisoned in a prison in Richmond.** She married Albert Miller, but didn't take his name. For several years she worked with feminist organizations.

Miranda Stuart was a woman who spent almost her entire life disguised as a man named James Barry. She entered Edinburgh College of Medicine as James, and upon graduating continued to pose as a male throughout her career in Britain's military service. She is responsible for the treatment of syphilis and gonorrhea, and she later became inspector general of all British hospitals in Canada.

Sara Josephine Baker was a medical inspector in the early 1900's. She was responsible for making a basic program of inspection for infectious diseases into a comprehensive approach to preventive health care for children. In her job she aided in the apprehension of Typhoid Mary Mallon.

Women have had to overcome many obstacles to fulfill their goals, but they have fought hard to overcome them. **Marie Zakrzewska** was forced to quit school at fourteen, but at twenty she went to a school for midwives. Later she was appointed chief midwife but opposition forced her to quit. She came to the U.S., learned English, and graduated from medical school. **She had to share office space with another doctor because landlords did not want to rent space to a woman.** Fortunately she persevered and founded the New England Hospital for women and children and her example contributed to the general acceptance of women physicians.

Clara Barton, founder of the American Red Cross, crossed battle lines to distribute supplies, search for the missing, and nurse the wounded. She devoted herself entirely to the organization, soliciting contributions and taking to the field with relief workers even as late as the Spanish-American War in Cuba, when she was seventy-seven. One outstanding achievement was her successful advocacy of the American amendment to the Geneva Convention in 1884, which permitted the Red Cross to provide relief in times of natural disasters and calamities as well as in wartime.

Agnodike was a Greek physician who disguised herself as a man in order to study medicine at a time when

16

Strong Role Models Throughout History

Athenian women were barred from practicing. Agnodike was revealed while delivering a baby for a woman who would not allow assistance until assured that the physician was a woman. She was brought to trial and would have been sentenced to death, but so many women protested that not only was she not executed, but the judge changed the law, therefore making it legal for women to practice medicine.

We have to ask ourselves why did it take so long?

- The Culinary Institute of America, in Hyde Park, New York, did not admit women to learn to become chefs until after 1970.

- Rudolph Virehow, a 19th century medical practitioner described women as "a pair of ovaries with a human being attached."

- Up to the 1970's, physicians were taught that morning sickness was caused by a woman's resentment of her condition.

- In 1993 **Julie Krone** won the Belmont Stakes to become the first woman jockey to win one of America's "Triple Crown" races. She was the third person in 126 years to win five races in one day at Saratoga. **Dorothy Tyler** paved the way in 1907 when she won a horse race in Joplin, Missouri, against experienced riders, and became America's first woman jockey.

- **Carol Moseley Braun** became the first black woman to the Senate in 1992. Her speech before the Senate led them to shred a flag-insignia patent held by the United Daughters of the Confederacy.

- **Janet Reno** became the first female U.S. attorney general. She was the first female state prosecutor in Dade County Florida and was re-elected five times.

- **Sheila Widnall** became the first woman secretary of the Air Force in 1993.

- **Tansu Ciller** became prime minister of Turkey in 1993. Two firsts- first woman to hold the post, first woman to lead an Islamic country without a family link to power.

"Unfortunately, there are still many women in the business world who refuse to support women. I call them "Honorary Males"- women who think that power is to be had only in the company of men. Women must realize they have found power, economic and political. Don't give your power away; use it for yourself and for the benefit of other women." Ginger Purdy

The great women before us worked so hard for the rights we have now, but we know that we have still so far to go. Each of us must feel a personal responsibility to fight for the right of each individual to have full expression of herself.

Spiritual Success

"God has given us two incredible things: absolutely awesome ability and freedom of choice. The tragedy is that, for the most part, many of us have refused them both."
Frank Donnelly

"God does not ask your ability or your inability. He asks only your availability."
Mary Kay Ash

Motivational books do not discuss the importance of spiritual growth in conjunction with success. It is hard to imagine one without the other when you realize that fulfilling your life's work is **the most important goal.** Knowing your life's purpose is inspiration from God. When a woman becomes conscious of her true self and spends her life in spiritual growth and in service, she will automatically become successful and find happiness in her life.

We can choose a life based on principles or right living that will permeate all the activities and time in our lives. **"We must pick something great to do, and do it. Never think of failure at all, for as we think now, that's what we get."** Maharishi Mahesk Yogi The greatness that we should aspire to is to live a life of **balance, growth, and service** in all the areas of our life: spiritual, mental, physical, and social. Our **"thoughts"** in all these areas should be focused on our interrelatedness. **"The happiness of your life depends on the quality of your thoughts."** Marcus Aurelius Antoninus. Everything that is a part of our lives, our families, our work, our relationships, our spirituality are a reflection of the choices and thoughts that we make from our inner (true) self.

How does knowing your true self affect your success? First, you will stop relying on information of mass thinking, believing and accepting what you see as the truth and then reacting with your emotions. Information has to be considered with logic, relevance, and validity, but it also has to be judged and compared to archetypal truths. Emotions are not to be determiners of our actions; they are *extensions of consciousness* and to be used to love our soul. When we rely on our emotions we are reacting to the fears and worries of our lives, or if they are happy emotions, we may not be seeing the truth of a situation.

Those who have chosen meditation and a transcending personality as a way to seek truth and meaning in life need to learn to use the insights and truths to understand their personality and how it is connected to ourselves. We are born with a pure self whose qualities are compassion, understanding, happiness, strength, patience, and love, but in our growth our true self is hidden by our identification with our environment, parents, experiences, habits or ideas about ourselves. Instead of fearing who we really are or declining the responsibility that comes hopefully with that knowledge, we should take time to find our true self.

Those who have tried psychotherapy, trying to understand and then resolve the unconscious conflicts that prevent our well-being, find that dwelling in the past is unproductive and depressing. Psychologists then use these findings as an excuse for us to behave the way we do. They have no explanation how one child grows up in poverty and decides to be successful, and another child grows up in the same conditions, becomes a robber. I would recommend that you look in your past to learn from the choices that you made. Often we find that our choices stemmed from the knowledge that we had at that time. If we had known other choices, perhaps we would have made them. If we had known our inner selves we would have relied on our own thinking. Or, we can seek what we learned from our choices. Asked to be totally honest in looking at past mistakes, most people will admit they knew they were making wrong choices, but did so anyway.

We sense feelings of hopelessness because of the emptiness in our lives. Hopefully sometime in our life we will decide that we want to grow up and find out what's missing or why we are not happy with our lives. Often to fill that emptiness we incorporate false beliefs, ideas, and feelings. We fill our physical bodies with food, alcohol, and drugs. Or we spend our time in self-gratification of underwork or overwork, and in wasted lives. It would have been great if all parents could have helped us develop our sense of worth, but if they didn't know their own, they couldn't pass that knowledge along. You now have the responsibility for knowing yourself.

How does the thinking of a woman relying on consciousness work? First, you know your position- a child of God. Living consciously means that you are **realistic, flexible, intuitive, independent, and creative.** You are open to change and correcting mistakes, and because you understand your interdependence, you are cooperative with others. Whatever label others try to apply, race, religious affiliation, locality, history or physical appearance, whatever memories you have of failures and whatever fears of failure you created are not applicable to who you really are. Motivational books stress that we seek goals that motivate us toward pleasure rather than pain. Our time is spent on seeking security, controlling others, avoiding fearful events, or seeking excitement and pleasure in life. We waste time and energy judging, criticizing, separating ourselves from others. How different our lives would be if we spent our energies on our own purpose, knowing that our decisions were correct because they were derived from God, and our hearts were in service of others. Minds can only think of one thought at a time, so if they are dwelling on the negative, they are not being creative.

You may act loving toward everyone, but you must keep negative people from sapping away your motivation and energy. Listen to their negative words about how bad the world is, how bad the economy is, how nobody is buying, and you will never be motivated to do anything. Also watch out for **dream stealers**. They have a negative reason why nothing will ever work out. Sometimes we are our own dream killers. We come up with all sorts of reasons why we don't think things will work out.

Become a thinker! Do your own thinking! Every fact or observation that becomes a part of your life and a source of your decision making needs to be judged, evaluated, or applied according to the truths of divine archetypes. *Use your intuitive knowledge. Be idealistic. Be creative and imaginative.* Create your world by utilizing the sayings: *If the mind can conceive of it, it can create it. Energy follows attention.*

"All things are created twice: first mentally, then physically. The key to creativity is to begin with the end in mind, with a vision and a blueprint of the desired result." Stephen R. Covey.

Golf great Jack Nicklaus in *Golf My Way*, said that **"successful people envision desired outcomes. They**

22

are not surprised by their achievements as they were already faultlessly executed in their minds."

A spiritual woman has an entrepreneurial heart because she is not bound by rules; her concept of the future is based on the possibility of things to come. She is seeking what is right rather than trying to control others.

When you talk to a spiritual person she will say that something wonderful is going on in our world today because she is living a life of awareness or consciousness. We can create our own world. **"Physical concepts are free creations of human mind and are not uniquely determined by the external world."** Albert Einstein

Self-awareness is looking within to find the answers to our thinking, past, present, and future, the roles we have chosen to play and the reason for our actions and habits. Our universe has been operating this way for all eternity, but many of us are just now tuning in. We are searching for our purpose in life. If you are one of these people, I ask, **"What is your plan for achieving a spiritual life and success thinking -success in the sense of fulfilling your purpose, living with the flow, not trying to control, becoming interconnected with the universe and humanity, and opening your mind to Quantum Thinking, unlimited thinking?"** When our thinking unifies, integrates, and looks in all directions at once, we are able to see insightfully with deep awareness.

"Success comes from knowing that you did your best to become the best you are capable of becoming."-John Wooden. You've seen or possibly you are one of those people who is **sleep walking through life**. You have no idea of the greatness that is within. Hopefully, each of us has experienced some time of greatness when we sank into our inner silence and learned to surrender to our true self, become whole through

23

connection, and transcendence to a greater place. We become people living in a state of awareness, mindfulness, or consciousness and overcome the negative forces of worry and fear which have been working against us. **"Worry,"** says Ed Foreman, **"is nothing less than the misuse of your imagination."** By using your God-given powers you focus on the correct direction of your life, and this is where we find the happiness we seek. We are to quit operating on the emotion-based response system and begin operating on the awareness or mindfulness system. Denis Waitley stated, *"Happiness cannot be traveled to, owned, earned, worn, or consumed. Happiness is the spiritual experience of living every minute with love, grace, and gratitude. "*

The business section of bookstores are reflecting our upswing interest in spirituality. Religious book sales have dramatically increased with several books such as the *Celestine Prophecy* and *Care of the Soul* remaining on the best sellers' list for months. Business books, such as Deepak Chopra's, *The Seven Spiritual Laws of Success* and *Creating Affluence*, suggest that laws from the Vedas, scriptural texts of Hinduism, give revelations about successful living.

However, most Americans are more knowledgeable as Christians with scriptures from the Holy Bible which direct our lives in successful living. In many cases our interpretations of these scriptures have been inaccurate or limited. **Deepak Chopra** believes that Western thought is behind in its thinking. On the contrary, I think Western thinking has gotten off track. The principles **Jesus Christ** taught us to live by have everything to do with successful living. He taught that we are to live in the world but be set apart. Christ preached a life that was not reactionary to our surroundings or other people. Our thinking is not to be based on our emotions, but from the truths God has revealed to us.

> *When I stand before God at the end of my life, I would hope that I would not have a single bit of talent left and could say, "I used everything you gave me."*
>
> Erma Bombeck

Biblical Laws for Success

1. Be Nonjudgmental

"Judge not, that ye be not judged. Matthew 7:1 *With what judgment ye judge, ye shall..."* Matthew 7:2 KJV *The Living Bible* says, *"For others will treat you as you treat them."* Matthew 7:1 LB *"Don't criticize and you won't be criticized. Judge not, and ye shall not be judged."* Luke: 6:37

Things are not good or bad; it is our choice about how we interpret them. The time we spend in judgment of others could be better spent thinking creatively. We spend too much time being too judgmental of ourselves. To be successful we must have faith in ourselves.

2. Live Life Abundantly

Christ said, *"I have come that you might have life and have it more abundantly."* John 10:10

"His life is the light that shines through the darkness, and the darkness can never extinguish it."
John 1:5

"...hear my voice...the voice of the son of God... and those who listen shall live" John 5:25

"...come to me so that I can give you this life..."
John 5:40

How do you know who you really are? How can you know how to live life abundantly? We are to live unlimited lives because we are full of potentiality. We are to discover our essential natures, not the labels and criticisms other have placed on us.

What are people talking about when they say to live in a state of consciousness or awareness? Living in a state of consciousness is not something that just happens. We make a personal, responsible choice about our guidance. As humans we have the ability to reason, to understand relationships.

Much has been said about "left brain" and "right brain" activities, but new findings show that there is more integration of our thinking than formerly thought. Women possess a larger connection between the two sides of the brain. We have a choice about whether to use our conscious, subconscious, or intuitive thinking to make a choice. We must make a conscious decision to use the knowledge we have when we make a rational or informed decision; it's not instinctive. We have a freedom of choice to be a thinking or nonthinking person. Hopefully, we will feel the responsibility of being a thinking person. We have independent will, which is our capacity to act. Joan Didion said, **"The willingness to accept responsibility for one's own life is the source from which self-respect springs."**

We do not have to be held captive to our past belief systems, our past behaviors, or our past history. Our **"victim thinking"** that we used to give ourselves excuses for not being responsible for our own lives can no longer be a part of our thinking. So much of our thinking is imprisoned with past thinking rather than present thinking or "living in the moment." Luci Swindoll believes, **"To experience happiness, we must train ourselves to live in this moment, to savor it for what it is, not running ahead in anticipation of some future date nor lagging behind in the paralysis of the past."** Mildred Barthel says, **"Happiness is a choice not an automatic response."** In retrospect and analysis of past mistakes, we can see where we made a conscious choice about suspending our awareness.

When we take a thought from our belief system, do we determine whether it came from our emotions, facts, or how we saw the interpretation what we thought happened? First, we must take an **active** rather than passive role in life. And that begins when we use our minds actively to **see our mistakes and correct them**, or **to seek out new knowledge and to be willing to question the truth about our old assumptions.** We use our minds to make abstractions, integration, and generalizations. People can choose meditation to get in touch with the silent spaces between their thoughts. Eastern philosophies often use mantras, a sound repeated to clear one's mind of thoughts. Using a mantra is not unchristian or going to send you to join the Moonies, it's just a device to clear your mind of thoughts. Eventually, you will find it even unnecessary.

Take time to concentrate on your spiritual, mental, and emotional levels before you challenge yourself with recreating your goals on the physical level. Everything you have been learning comes into interplay in your daily life. When you are seeking your purpose, look to the things you like to do naturally and that come to you easily. The innate knowledge, skills, talents and interests you have been developing along with your people connections and activities draw you to your higher purpose.

When we take on our life's purpose, we need to decide if our goals, time and energies are being spent correctly in pursuit of that purpose. After all, fulfilling your higher purpose is not just doing a job, it is **who you are**- your energy, personality, and physical form. **"My research offers impressive evidence that we feel better when we attempt to make our world better...to have a purpose beyond one's self lends to existence a meaning and direction-the most important characteristic of high well-being."** -Gail Sheehy

Commitment to purpose enables us to face oncoming difficulties. Consciousness heightens our psychic senses of vision, hearing, feeling, and knowing, so that we can learn

28

through solving problems, actually seeing them as stepping stones to new understandings and beliefs. **"The secret of happiness is not discovered in the absence of trials, but in the midst of them."** Ted Nace

We find that using our minds brings new joy into our lives because we grow in understanding of the world around us, and equally important we grow in understanding our own needs, hopes, and feelings. We are able to distinguish our motives as seeking pain or happiness.

Paul said in the *Bible* that we are to pray unceasingly. Only recently did I understand how we could do this. When we live in a state of consciousness or awareness we are **"in the world"** as the *Bible* says, but we are **"not of this world."** Our praying unceasingly means that we are aware of our connection with God, our interconnection with other humans, animals, and plants. We are a part of the whole universe and therefore able to know its wisdom.

Living in a state of consciousness or awareness means that you are:

Thinking-
You perceive with clarity
You observe with reality
You make judgments from the facts
You are open to new knowledge
You are rational and logic
You choose to live in a state of consciousness
Focusing-
You are persistent
You are loyal
You are seeking consistency
You respect truth
You are honest
You are willing to confront your self
You are willing to see and correct your errors

3. Seek the desires of your heart

Naomi Stephen says in *Finding Your Life's Mission*, **"Your first obligation is to carry out the mission you are meant for, not what your father, mother, mate or friends say you should do. Your mission will manifest in you when you decide to listen to your heart's desire."** **Audrey Hepburn** was successful as a stage and screen actress, but her work as a goodwill ambassador for the United Nations Children's Fund showed her heart's desire. **"Success is courageously living each moment as fully as possible. Success means the courage to flow, struggle, change, grow, and all other contradictions of the human conditions. Success means being true to you."** Dr. Tom Rusk and Dr. Randy Read

Linda Lewis started her business selling plants out of the back of her Volkswagen bus. She now owns a business that is bringing in sales of $2 million. Her business is gradually spreading across the world. She does interior plantscapes on a grand scale for casinos. She recreated an elaborate rain forest for the Mirage Hotel's opening, complete with arching palms, misty waterfalls, and exotic foliage imported from Asia.

When **Paul Keene** met **Gandhi** during a trip to India in 1938 the guru told him that the secret to success in life was "to give away everything you have." So Keene gave up his college teaching position and then he and his wife spent nearly five years learning organic farming. With a $5,000 loan they purchased Walnut Acres, a farm outside Harrisburg, Pennsylvania.

The couple sold their produce to make extra money. A food writer at the **New York Herald Tribune** wrote an article about the farm after eating some of their apple butter. People started sending letters requesting their food and today the business is a $ 7 million dollar mail order business. The two policies which helped their business the most were a profit-sharing program and cross-training employees. When crops are growing, the employees work on them and in the winter they move them inside to filling orders in the mail order department.

Marsha Sinetar in *To Build the Life You Want, Create the Work You Love* and *Do What You Love, The Money Will Follow,* suggests that you must re-focus to start a business or change careers. First, she asks, "Was there a time when you really loved what you did? What lifelong interests do you have?" Many people are choosing careers based on their hobbies and interests. She suggests that you take a spiritual approach to changing your outlook toward work.

4. Give To Others

We should strive for financial independence so that we can fulfill our purpose in life without worrying about next month's bills. Our minds are to do unlimited thinking rather than worrying. We know that the universe is unlimited and because we are a part of that universe, we too are unlimited. Scientists say that our universe could be multiplied 100 million times and still not fill the universes of the Milky Way. Our world is truly unlimited. Dr. Robert Schuller, past of the Hour of Power, helped change my attitude about money.

5. What Ye Sow So Shall Ye Reap

What you send out, you will get back. Listen to your "gut feelings." You receive this information in your solar plexus, located at the front of the body, extending from the top of the diaphragm to just below the navel. This is where many of our nerves come together.

How many times have you looked back and thought that you gave up too soon. We are to persevere. *"For after a while we will reap a harvest of blessing if we don't get discouraged and give up."* Gal. 6:9

6. The Law of Detachment

"Don't worry about things...for you already have life and a body- and they are far more important." Matthew 6:25

I think that this is one of the hardest concepts for us to understand. People who live with the flow of life have a sense of detachment. This means that they do not have expectations of people, actions, or events. Without expectations you are non-judgmental of people's behaviors; therefore, you are not reactive to their praise or criticism. Detachment from material possessions frees you to concentrate on the important things in life. Everything is in its proper perspective. You lose the desire to be competitive, jealous, selfish, and worried about losing your possessions. Detachment gives you a freedom you never experienced before and allows you to give full expression of yourself.

7. Fulfill Your Purpose

"Don't hide your light! Let it shine for all."
Matthew 5:15

"No one lights a lamp and hides it! Instead, he puts it on a lampstand to give light to all who enter the room."
Luke 11:33

God has chosen you for a specific purpose that no one else can fulfill. Wow! What responsibility, yet what freedom from competition, worries, doubts. When you know what you are doing is the **right thing** then you don't have to answer to your parents, spouse, or children.

The choices we make about morals, responsibility, and conscious living affect our self esteem. The actions we take in response to our thinking determine for how we feel about ourselves. You must have evidence that supports your thinking of self worth. You can't think one way and act another way.

"And we know that all that happens to us is working for our good if we love God and are fitting into his plans."
Romans 8:28

Jenny Craig says **"It's not what you do once in a while, it's what you do day in and day out that makes the difference."**

Jesus said, **"I am the Light of the World"**John 9:5. We are asked to be lights in our world. Margaret Fuller advises *"If you have knowledge, let others light their candles at it."* Carl Jung said, **"As far as we can discern, the sole purpose of human existence is to kindle a light in the darkness of mere being."** As a matter of fact, physicists now

33

say that we are made up of light. It is now known that atoms can be split into smaller particles of which we can not find the tiniest part. Astrophysicist, **Stephen Hawking** notes the forces described as wavelengths of electromagnetism, or light are the building blocks of matter. People who have experienced (NDE) Near Death Experiences describe those they encounter and their own images to be made of light.

We are spirits who have bodies, but our bodies nor our egos are to rule over us. The ego presents our false self and its information will only hurt us. We see what we expect and we invite in our expectations. We know ourselves as mind, born in the image of God and this is how we know the Truth.. We know nothing outside of ourselves. If you perceive your body as your reality and set limits to what you believe, you will be lonely and unhappy. Choose to live a life of greatness. Give yourself that gift. and make decisions that reflect your greatness and show how you value yourself. God asks only that you believe and then He will show you how easy it is to accomplish your purpose. Learn to decide with God by letting the Holy Spirit communicate with your mind. You have taught yourself not to communicate with God. Ask to remember the perfect relationship you had with God before you were born. You are not helpless in God's presence. You can be happy in this world you have created because it is based on guilt and fear. You not longer need to attack yourself or others. Give yourself and others love because that is all there is and when you do this you will become strong. You will no longer feel the sense of loss and then will no longer fear. Who are you going to believe, God's evaluation of you or your ego's?

When God spoke the words, *"Let there be light in the darkness,"* it made us understand that the brightness in his glory is seen in the face of Jesus Christ. We are also a reflection of his glory. Our bodies are a precious treasure of light and power that now shines within us. Though our bodies are a perishable container, everyone can see that the glorious power within must be from God and is not our own.

"Ask, and you will be given what you ask for. Seek, and you will find. Knock, and the door will be opened. For everyone who asks, receives. Anyone who seeks, finds. If only you will knock , the door will open." Matthew 7:7

Learn to make affirmation a way of life. They lift you above the attitude of resignation that renders you helpless victims of the winds of circumstance and luck. It is an opportunity to assume control of your own life and design the world you want.

I asked my friend **Linda Johnson** to write about one of her experiences with affirmations. She wrote, it was late in 1990 when I was introduced to the man, who is now my husband, to the law of manifesting through affirmations. Affirmations were so second nature to my life by that time that I used them for everything I wanted from parking places to a new home. Rich treated my ideas on Universal law in much the same way an indulgent father treats his child's imaginary friend. I have always felt that sharing anything so important, life-changing and personal should be done only when a person is ready and receptive so I had never really discussed my beliefs with him in depth.

Rich is a salesman and his product is primarily high tech equipment for monitoring air emissions from manufacturing. The company he was representing was bidding on a job that was falling under the mandates of the new federal "Clean Air" act and they were a virtual David in a field of Goliaths. The competition were larger and more established in the industry and looked upon this new interloper as no real threat.

The bid process took months. Laws and guidelines had to be strictly adhered to and specifications had to be honed to a fine edge before the quote process could even begin. It was a tremendous risk for Rich and his company to expend so much time and effort working on a job in which they were, at best, a long shot, I could see the pressure getting to him and he became tense and moody. He would come home from the road mentally exhausted and without the enthusiasm and confidence that were his style.

The affirmation was written in the present tense and was short succinct, as all affirmations should be:

--(company name) -- serves -- (client name) --
efficiently, professionally and successfully
to their mutual benefit.

I wrote it on 3x5 index cards and taped them to the bathroom mirror, the refrigerator, over the kitchen sink and on his pillow. He couldn't walk ten feet in any direction without seeing one. He was amused when he first saw them but, in his desperation, he began asking me how affirmations were supposed to work (the old "any port in a storm" approach).

I explained that the energy created by a positive idea in the computer of your mind, nurtured by a conviction and acceptance on an inner level, must manifest on the physical plane. No builder would ever construct a house without a set of blueprints. No master chef could attempt to create a gourmet meal without a menu or recipe. Designing your perfect world and putting the design into words, sets in motion mental energy that is incomprehensibly powerful. We both began using the affirmation... seeing it, repeating it aloud and with conviction several times a day. It became a reality in our minds.

In October, I received a late night phone call from Rich who was at an industry show in South Carolina. During a cocktail party, he had overheard a competitor telling a group of colleagues that he had just received verbal confirmation of his company's award of he bid. It was the worst possible news for Rich. My reaction was to laugh. Before a goal is reached, there is always a test of faith. Having been through it so many times, I was not surprised, but his faith was shaken to the core. I told him to put the conversation out of his mind and continue to affirm his success- no matter how difficult it was to feel it.

Six weeks later, when little "David" received written confirmation of the bid award, the industry was shell shocked. This time, my phone call from the road was ecstatic. Rich said he would be home that evening to prepare for the major celebration. When he walked in, I handed him a gift. The amazement in his eyes when he saw the small bronze plaque was with his affirmation engraved on it was delicious. I had ordered it the morning after his frantic phone call from South Carolina.

The secret of the affirmation is simple. You must believe with all your heart and against all odds and evidence to the contrary that you can achieve your goal and manifest your desires. You must be patient. You must be sure that you are not wishing for something that is wrong for you or injurious to someone else. You must recognize that the "Source" of your power is the same creative force that designed your mind with all of its unlimited potential.

There are those who believe that I am the luckiest person who ever walked the face of the earth. But those who know me well, know that I have been blessed with the knowledge that transcends "luck" and denies chance. If you are one of those people who would like to change your circumstances and establish more control over your life, try affirmations for one month. My husband would be the first to guarantee your success.

8. Use the Gifts God Has Given You

God has given us different gifts and abilities. Some of us think that because we can not sing, paint, or be athletic that we do not have gifts. 1 Corinthians 12:4-7 of the *Living Bible* says, *"Now God gives us many kinds of special abilities, but it is the same Holy Spirit who is the source of them all. There are different kinds of service to God, but it is the same Lord we are serving. There are many ways in which God works in our lives, but it is the same God who does the work in and through all of us who are his. The Holy Spirit displays God's power through each of us as a means of helping the entire church."*

The following verses list the different kinds of gifts. 1 Corinthians 12:8-10 says, *"To one person the Spirit gives the ability to give wise advice, someone else may be especially good at studying and teaching, and this is his gift from the same spirit. He gives special faith to another, and to some one else the power to heal the sick. He gives power for doing miracles to some, and to others power to prophesy and preach."*

How does a person with the ability to prophesy get the information? God has given us the psychic abilities in the areas of intuition, seeing, hearing, and feeling. We all have ESP abilities, which some of us have developed or been made more aware of. Ron Dalrymple, author of *The Inner Manager,* (Quantum Psychology Press) says that **"people who rely on rational analysis aren't getting the whole picture. They are blocking out valuable information and insight."**

Psychic intuition is the most unlimited of the psychic senses. This is the ability to "just know" about a situation or be warned about the future. It makes you a more effective decision maker and better entrepreneur. Because psychic intuition is only based on a feeling that may not last long and have no other supporting evidence, you must learn to trust these feelings. Everett Suters, author of *The Unnatural Act of Management,* recalled reading *The IBM Way*, which described IBM management style and reflected Suter's way of running his business. Suters, a former IBM employee turned entrepreneur, noted that he picked up these thoughts intuitively. Intuition, he says, often appears unnatural and is better than instinct.

Psychic intuition offers us advantages in our business and personal life because it helps us anticipate problems and make adjustments to changing circumstances. The intuitive person is innovative, creative, and resists restrictions. We use our intuition more often than we think.

Some people receive information in the form of extrasensory signals such as sounds or words. Audients are people who have abilities in psychic hearing. They are very analytical people who want to be sure of what they hear so that they can make correct decisions. Through key guide words they are able to analyze problems or situations. They have the ability to hear when someone is lying and they can transmit psychic thoughts.

Psychic hearing is the hardest of the psychic abilities to develop and often the person doubts their own potential. They may ask too many questions or not trust their own feelings or intuition. I have finally learned to trust the small voice that comes to me because it has always proven right.

Recently, I was about to leave on a speaking engagement when a voice told me to "take a hat". I love hats but forget to wear them, yet I went back into the house to get one for the trip. My speaking engagement was The Mad Hatters Luncheon attended by 450 women wearing hats for a contest!

Other people are stronger in psychic vision. They can naturally see what is wrong with something because they can visualize situations, problems and solutions in their minds.

Because their world is visual, they are great color coordinators, great at seeing how things go together, and they are into planning their time and sensing the correct way to get somewhere. Unfortunately, they tend to be worriers seeing what might go wrong and perfectionists because they want everything right.

How can you know if you are a visionary? Are you more aware of the things around you like scenic views, do you prefer uncovered windows, lots of light. You resist change because you know how you want everything to be so before you make a decision, you take a long time to think about it or sleep on it.

Lastly, the people who are high in psychic feeling are more sensitive to the feelings of others. They are great friends to have because they give of themselves and are more flexible because they are more concerned that other people are happy. They are the huggers who look out for your safety, and are good listeners to others problems.

My friend, **Mary Charles Watts**, is very strong in psychic feeling. She becomes sad at times for no reason and then realizes that she is picking up other people's feelings. She appears overly emotional at times and becomes overwhelmed by her feelings. But now that she has studied why she acts this way, she is better able to cope with her feelings.

If you are married or date a feeler, you need to be more careful of hurting their feelings because they pick up on your moods and words so intensely. Fortunately, they forgive easily. Most of us should try to increase our psychic abilities in this area.

Bruce Goldsmith is an example of someone with psychic intuition. His family owned the 64-year-old Baronet Coffee Inc. in Hartford, Connecticut. The company sold coffee by mail order and wholesale. Individual bags were sold in the back of the factory, but Bruce had a gut feeling that a retail store located in the factory would do well. He went against logic but relied on the knowledge he had picked up in the business. After observing his customers, he felt that they would like to buy their coffee directly from the source. Retail sales have since quadrupled.

Gordon Gould, who spent 30 years seeking the patents for his inventions in the field of lasers, fought legal battles with corporate opponents. Gould awoke during the early hours of November 9, 1957, and envisioned the entire laser process. He wrote notes and made sketches about the invention. For several days he was able to visualize all the future possible uses for lasers. He had the forethought to have a notary public date and stamp his paperwork because other inventors and corporations sought patent rights later.

However, Gould made the mistake of listening to an attorney who was not competent in his field. Despite this, he paid the attorney $500,000 in the end as he had promised. Our government, which needed the new laser technology, withdrew a $1 million dollar grant because when Gould was younger he and his girlfriend attended a course on Marxism. The inventor went to court many times over the 30 years to receive his patents. During his lifetime Gould is expected to make around $60 million for his patents.

A person strong in psychic intuition may get diverted by all the thoughts and ideas they create. Learning more about my intuitiveness helps me understand why I read several books at a time or work on various projects at one time. The more excited I get about new knowledge, the faster I begin to talk. Additionally, I am a visual person, which means that I picture things in my head before I can get the words out. Many times I will get bored in the middle of a sentence and simply go on to the next idea.and leave the listener wondering what happened. I met a speech therapist in

Mobile, Alabama, who talked just like me. I asked her how she was able to do her job. She makes a conscious effort to slow down so that people will understand what she is saying.

The **Bible** says in 1 Thessalonians 5:20-21, *"Do not scoff at those who prophesy, but test everything that is said to be sure it is true."* We can predict the future, but we also know that since we are able to choose, our futures may change. We can know about future actions, decisions, and situations. We are able to see many of these problems find their own solutions. Dr. Wayne Dyer says our lives are a sum total of the choices we have made.

How do you go about doing this?

1. **Bring your problem or decision to mind.**
2. **Make a list of your choices.**
3. **Review each choice**
4. **Shift your thinking upward to your Intuition Psychic Reception Area, located at the top of the head. The central fissure of the brain is the most direct path to the corpus collosum, which has been in the news lately, because they think it is larger in women than in men. It is a massive group of nerves which connects the two hemispheres of the brain which means that women have an advantage of shifting the right and left sides of the brain.**
5. **When you shift your awareness to this area you increase your alpha-brain-wave activity and thus increase your extrasensory ability.**
6. **You can choose to be intuitive any time you need to make a decision about any subject, person or action.**

Traveling to different and unfamiliar cities to do book signings used to be more difficult for me though I have a map, I do not have a navigator to figure out the streets while I am driving. I have learned to access my intuitive abilities and actually make choices that feel which is the best way to get to my location. I have talked to salespeople who travel all day and they rely on their intuitiveness for directions.

People who have developed their intuitiveness are more exciting to be around because they are interested in everything going on around them. Norman Vincent Peale said, **"Nothing gives such complete and profound happiness as the perpetually fresh wonder and mystery of exciting life."**

I tend to drive my friends crazy at times because when ideas come to my mind, I talk very rapidly about them. I write the thoughts down or I'll lose them. My friend Anne gets perturbed at me because I reply "uh-huh" frequently while we talk. She doesn't know that I really do know what she is going to say. She is a highly organized person who does linear thinking, but when she has a problem to solve, she asks me for solutions.

Loida Lewis, head of TLC Beatrice, starts each day reading scriptures and meditating for 45 minutes. Her husband died in 1993 of a brain tumor, and she believes her faith helped her cope with her husband's death. Her chief of operations describes Loida as demanding as her husband, but more **intuitive**. She is a lady of intelligence and skills and a person who makes decisions people can respect.

Refinancing of the company was delayed a year because Loida followed Philippine tradition and mourned for a year. TLC is the world's largest African-American-owned business with revenues of $985 million!

When minority stockholders revolted, she offered a cash-out option and allowed a secondary public offering.

This risk-taking move produced sales of $1.82 billion in 1994. A Harvard law degree, working as an immigration attorney, and then a full-time adviser for her husband prepared her to later take over the business.

Our interconnectedness offers us a successful life in business, personally, physically, mentally, and emotionally when we draw closer to each other. We find that having close friendships lead to a stronger immune system functioning, lower levels of cholesterol, more hopeful results after cancer, and lower death rates among heart patients. Having someone to talk to is very powerful medicine. Studies have shown that patients who belong to support groups regain their health or live longer than those who isolate themselves.

Husbands and wives should be become *interdependent*. Besides the obvious facts of life, many spouses die or get divorced. When you place all your faith in another person, he or she will do the human thing and fail you. You must be **PROACTIVE, RESPONSIBLE FOR YOUR OWN LIFE.** While women are almost three times as likely as men to suffer from depression, **William Rhodes,** a psychologist at Texas A & M University, found that women attending college full or part time were much less likely to suffer depression.

9. **Do unto others as you would have them do unto you.**

All of us can quote this scripture, but do we put it into action? Think of how different out world would be if we functioned according to this spiritual law in all areas of our lives. Because many people are not living by this spiritual law, a new outcry has been heard for social responsibility. It is being given more attention by the media, awards, education, books on the subject, and membership organizations.

10. Love One Another

We show our love for others when we speak, act, and think with:

kindness - The way you want people to treat you is directly reflective of the way you treat them. As your spirituality grows, you will become more connected with everyone. As the **Bible** says, "What man would hurt **himself?**" Our concern for others will grow as we see our interrelatedness. Awareness teaches us to listen to our words, our tone, facial demeanor, and to watch our body language.

For a man's heart determines his speech. A good man's speech reveals the rich treasures within him. Mattthew 12:35-36.

patience - Take time to listen to the other person. Carefully monitor your body movements so that you reflect a patient attitude. Remember that what you are thinking is reflected in your face, so take time to be meditative and relaxed. All of us have stored harsh words in our memories because someone spoke too quickly and didn't think about what he or she was saying.

humility - The less we concentrate on acquiring possessions, and the more we see ourselves as spirits with bodies, the more humility we will express. Our purpose is not self-promotion but service. As we begin to see the big cosmic picture, we are grateful for the gift of living unlimited lives full of potentiality.

generosity - This quality naturally follows humility. When we take the responsibility for our lives and learn to live following God's plan, then we will have a more generous attitude. Life will not be such a struggle because we will know how to make the right decisions, how to interact in our relationships, and not be reactive, emotionally controlled beings. We will be generous in our praises, love, care, and selflessness.

respect - When we love and respect ourselves, then we are able to love and respect others to the same degree. We acknowledge the equality of all people to have self worth. When you open yourself to see the other person's position, you can more easily understand why he acts that particular way. Again, your actions, words, and thinking reflects the respect you have for someone.

11. Your "fruits" will show your labors

From Matthew: 12:33 we learn that a tree is identified by its fruit. Christ was walking down a road when he saw a tree that was not producing. At his word, the tree shriveled up and died because it was serving no purpose. Polls say that 40 million people watched the O. J. Simpson trial. When the trial is over, what fruits can these people say they have produced?

A second story from the **Bible** talks about the necessity to prune a tree to encourage new growth. Fruits and flowers are produced on the new growth. I had some crepe myrtle trees that disappointed me every year because they did not bloom. The year I finally took the time in the fall to cut them back was when I had beautiful blooms that spring. We have to constantly "prune" our lives and take out the time wasters, negative attitudes, destructive habits, and false beliefs that are destroy our fruits.

You can Make People Believe Anything- Unfortunately

My cousin Freddy recently asked me, *the motivational speaker,* if I really believed all that stuff about motivation! Of course I do! Look at all the things that people are made to believe, good and bad. Freddy has worked for the state government all his life and says he is unhappy with his job. When asked why he doesn't make a career change or change the attitude about his job, he says he doesn't know what he wants to do. But he is doing nothing about seeking other options, about broadening his thinking, or finding his purpose.

Women have been told throughout time that they are by nature submissive, too emotional, weak, and responsible for nurturing everyone else. Some continue to play the subservient role in a male dominated society. They don't look at their strengths and potentials.

Look at how cults can influence the minds of followers and attract people who are willing to leave their homes, friends, and jobs to turn over their power to a leader who tells them it's all right for him to have multiple wives and to have children with each of them while they are not permitted to have sex with their own spouse. The leader convinces his followers that the world is against them and they must defend themselves no matter the cost.

Look at the roles women play in the movies- most of them!! I tuned in a movie about **professional** women who were bemoaning their problems with men. One said "Let's go shopping after work," and the other one said, "I can't because I already spent $600 at lunch trying to forget about (whomever)." The conversation ended with a quote about a woman who was choosy about whom she married and then the remorseful words ".....and then the men quit asking." Awareness is taking issue with these stupid roles, thoughtless commercials, and routine ways of thinking. Women have been led to believe that if they act and think effectively they will ruin their chances for a satisfying emotional relationship, a responsible job, and satisfying life. Such thinking has caused women to believe that their strongest assets are really liabilities.

Women have been encouraged to concentrate on the emotions and reactions of others so that they have been diverted from examining and expressing their own emotions. They wake up after the children or maybe their husband is gone and ask "Who am I?" They have spent so much time as subordinates, attuned to the various moods, pleasure, and displeasure of those around them that they have not learned who they are. We are not teaching our sons and daughters that they are responsible for their feelings. This does not mean emotional outbursts and uncontrolled reactions. It means awareness and responsibility for changing attitudes. Women are more willing to feel and tolerate their feelings which is good, but it does not mean that we have to tolerate the false beliefs about our self worth. Women have a right and obligation to refuse to be used as an object, either commercially or in intimate personal encounters, to be demeaned in any kind of relationship, and to continue the role of subordinate.

The changes in our world in the last few years, the crumbling of the Berlin Wall and the Soviet Union, the Communist reign of China that now sees the benefits of our capitalistic society and is building $650,000 homes for government officials, says that the false thinking about the role of women can be changed. The United States did not change the Soviet Union's thinking. The revolution was from within. And this is the same place that women will initiate change.

Listen to the words that you personally use about yourself that reflect your inner thinking. I have gotten into the habit of describing myself as passive despite the loud outcries of my friends. The truth is that I **was passive** in some areas in the past, but I continue to say the same old phrases. Let's all re-examine what we are saying and thinking about ourselves and take responsibility for who we really are.

Success Through Spirituality For Women

My friend Penny has made remarkable changes in her life by starting her own graphics business and she now has a sense of direction. But she has the problem of "lack of sense of direction" when she is drives to meet with clients. Penny would like to live in a dream world where women shouldn't have to start fires, clean cars, or do lawn work because that's a man's job. The reality is that she chooses not to be married so she must take responsibility for these areas. She laughs at all the times she has forgotten where she parked her car at the mall and has to walk around the lot searching. Recently, though, as she grows in spirituality and responsibility, her sense of awareness is growing. She no longer jumps out of her car without observing the aisle or row, which entrance she took to the store, and identifying markers. You may laugh, but look at your own lack of awareness. How many times do people say negative remarks about the race or nationality or sex of others that you do not register or respond? How many times do your words reflect the weak, undirected life your are living? How do your actions demonstrate your lack of growth and responsibility?

Bern has lived across the street from me for 17 years and is now 25 and works installing dishwashers. He complains that his boss, an alcoholic, yells and cusses at him. When I ask him why he doesn't quit and start his own business, he says, "I don't want the responsibility of getting the jobs." So he stays in a job making less money and being mistreated. The odd thing is that Bern has spent hundreds of dollars on motivational tapes which he kindly lets me borrow, but he doesn't put his knowledge into action.

An article in a current magazine derides insurance companies because they do not want to insure women who have physically abusive husbands or they want to charge them higher rates, like race car drivers, because they may permit someone to injure them. The insurance companies say that the women have a choice about their injuries. Neither the writer of the article or apparently the insurance companies has done anything to change the thinking of these women that they don't have to be objects of mistreatment.

The power that we have to change our minds is unlimited. Look at the examples of the number of people who believed that a major restaurant chain was serving horse meat or the teenagers who wear their clothes several sizes too big because someone wanted to start a new fad. We have actually gotten so used to seeing pants that are nearly falling off, pockets located at the knees, and intelligent kids who choose to look stupid by wearing their hats backwards that now we don't even look.

How does your child's school recognize the students who do well academically? Are they ever singled out with special jackets with letters on them? Dr. Betty Hamburg says, **"We've speeded up the clock without being very helpful to adolescents. We teach them about fallopian tubes but very little about the meaning of relationships and responsibility toward others."** If someone had suggested teaching values in schools a few years ago, there would have been a great uproar. But with violent crimes up 575% since 1960, illegitimacy up from 5% in 1960 to 30% in 1995, and 30 million abortions since Roe v. Wade, parents, teachers, and society realize that we are not teaching right from wrong or a value system.

My friend Anne said that she worked at a hospital that rewarded the doctors who turned in their paperwork on time by giving them a carnation to wear in their jacket lapel. Doctors who did outstanding work were recognized in the newsletter. She noted how the problems with paperwork were eliminated and how happy the doctors were to be given individual recognition.

Spiritual Growth Leads to Success

"The historic period in which we live is a period of reawakening to a commitment to higher values, a reawakening of individual purpose, and a reawakening of the longing to fulfill that purpose in life."

Robert Fritz, *The Path of Least Resistance*

Success

"Success has a price tag on it, the tag reads **COURAGE, DETERMINATION, RISK TAKING, PERSEVERANCE** and **CONSISTENCY -- DOING** the right things for the **RIGHT REASONS** and not just when we feel like it."

James M. Meston

The less you worry about your reputation of failure, the more success you will accomplish.

"You are free to choose, but the choices you make today will determine what you will have, be, and do in the tomorrow of your life."

Zig Zigler

Just as there is abundance in our universe, there is abundance in our world. Businesses and people need to learn that there are no limits to the success and money they can acquire. Myopic thinking keeps them from seeing the whole picture. They spend negative time

51

focusing on problems instead of alternative solutions. Many individuals see problems and solutions as only having only two alternative choices. **"The business of expanding your consciousness is not an option. Either you are expandable or you are expendable."** Rev. Robert Schuller

The next step is to make assumptions about these alternative choices. We can not only look at them through our own eyes, but through the perspective of buyers, employers, and co-workers. When we achieve this interdependent thinking in our organizations, relationships and businesses, we are able to work and live with synergy. This is when creative imaginations are combined and thus produce more solutions or ideas than each person working individually. It is said ideas are like rabbits. You get a couple and learn how to handle them, and pretty soon you have a dozen. We are all blessed with creative imagination to establish in our minds the way we think things should be and how to overcome the problems we see now.

Carl Rogers says, **"If I can listen to what he tells me, if I can understand how it seems to him, then I will release potent forces of change within him."** And finally, David Augsburgur says, **"To love you as I love myself is to seek to hear you as I want to be heard and understand you as I long to be understood."**

> **"I can't imagine a person becoming a success who doesn't give this game of life everything he's got."**
> Walter Cronkite

52

Purpose

Many of us don't seek our purpose because we know its discovery will create demand and desire which we're too lazy to fulfill. Elaine Maxwell challenged herself, " **My will shall shape my future. Whether I fail or succeed shall be no man's doing but my own. I am the force; I can clear any obstacle before me or I can be lost in the maze. My choice, my responsibility, win or lose, only I hold the key to my destiny."** We would rather become stale and suffer disappointment in our present comfort zone than to surpass the limitations we have placed upon ourselves. *Our actions indicate our purpose.* **"Purpose, or mission, is determined by the development of values, balance, ethics, humor, morality, and sensitivities. It manifests itself in the way we look at life."** Luci Swindoll Most people are seeking pleasure out of life first instead of their purpose. The result is that they will never have lasting happiness. Dick Verneil, speaking about commitment believes, **"If you don't invest very much, then defeat doesn't hurt very much and winning is not very exciting."**

Addis Gezahegen grew up in Ethiopia where her childhood was filled with disappointment and poverty. Her father died when she was in the 6th grade, and her struggling mother couldn't afford to keep her in school. However, Addis utilized the gifts God gave her as she ran through the rugged mountains of Ethiopia in her bare feet and became the first woman marathon runner to represent Ethiopia in the Olympics.

Tom Flores noted, **"A total commitment is paramount to reaching the ultimate in performance."** Do you think it was fun for **Janet Evans** to get up at 4:45 a.m. six days a week to swim 6,000 meters before school and then do another workout after school? We watched her win three gold medals at the Olympics, but we didn't realize the preparation and sacrifice she made to get there. Here's her winning philosophy:

"While we are here we should set goals and achieve them, make the best of things, make others feel good about themselves, and be happy with what we are and what we are doing." Janet Evans

Throughout history many times when women became good at sports or other achievements, men put up obstacles to keep down their accomplishments. Because women started winning car races, they were no longer allowed to enter. **Hazel Hotchkiss Wightman,** who was born in 1886 had to rise at dawn to practice on the tennis courts because they were closed to women at 8 a.m.. She went on to win the national Womens' Singles, Doubles, and Mixed Doubles.

Bessie Coleman was denied a pilot's license in the U.S. because instructors refused to teach a black woman. She moved to France and became an excellent pilot. Bessie later returned to the U.S. but died when she was thrown from her plane while practicing for an air show.

Marian Wright Edelman has always found her purpose to be children's rights. She founded the Washington Research Project and the Children's Defense Fund. She published in 1992 *The Measure of Our Success: A Letter to My Children and Yours* . She said, **"If you don't like the way the world is, you change it. You have an obligation to change it. You just do it one step at a time."**

Mary White Ovington was a social worker and reformer who lived from 1865-1951. She was a civil rights advocate who sparked the founding of the National Association for the Advancement of Colored People in 1909 and served as its chairman for four decades because she saw the potential of her people.

No matter what your age, you can still fulfill your purpose in life. **Clara Hale,** better known as Mother Hale, retired in 1969 and then founded Harlem's Hale House, an African-American child-care provider which grew into one of the nation's highest respected child-care institutions. She died in 1992 but her work still goes on.

Learn to get in touch with silence within yourself and know that everything in this life has a purpose.   There are no mistakes, no coincidences, all events are blessings given to us to learn from.   Elizabeth Kubler-Ross

---

Judith Jamison is a magnificent dancer who has performed with the American Ballet Theater on Broadway, and was a star dancer of the Alvin Ailey Company.   The Jamison Project was her own modern-dance group, but in 1989 she became artistic director of the Alvin Ailey Dance Group when Ailey died.

"Don't let other people define your creative potential. No one including you, knows what you are capable of doing or thinking up."
                    Dr. Michael LeBoeuf

Potential

"There is no such thing as can't, only won't. If you're qualified, all it takes is a burning desire to accomplish, to make a change. Go forward, go backward. Whatever it takes! But you can't blame other people or society in general. It all comes from your mind. When we do the impossible we realize we are special people." Jan Ashford

Anyone from America who travels Europe marvels because most people there can speak several languages. Most Americans have taken a foreign language in school, but have forgotten the vocabulary with disuse. From this we learn that other cultures are not smarter, they then give more attention to other languages. The mind has the ability to learn and retain several languages, and when a child grows up in dual cultures, he can easily speak two or more languages.

With this in mind, think about how we get bound and encircled by our cultures, religions, beliefs, understanding, and language. I have a friend who came to the U.S. 12 years ago and is a member of a very strict religious sect. He is very critical of other religions and spirituality so he limits his thinking by seeing only his beliefs as true. I point out to him that if we both had been adopted, we would be speaking another language, eating different foods, and having different cultural values. And this knowledge should give us new insights about God.

Have you ever marveled that God understands and hears all the languages of the world? Or that He is more accepting of all the beliefs and different religions? We choose our religious beliefs because that is where we are at that time. The more that I read and meditate, the more enlightened and unlimited my faith becomes. It is a marvelous growing process. When we realize that our minds, too, have the ability to learn any of the world's languages we can marvel at our abilities and understand our connection with God. We know that we only use 10% of our mental abilities, and we reflect on our limited exploration of other languages. Then we think of all the other areas of learning we neglect and all the *possibility* thinking.

We grew up with the belief that people who studied and work in math and science were more intelligent. However, there are different kinds of intelligence: conceptual, intuitive, musical, imaginative, spiritual, physical, emotional, intellectual, and social. When we become non-judgmental of ourselves and others, we will quit worrying about comparing and competing and concentrate on succeeding with our special gifts.

"You can have the faith to move mountains," the **Bible** tells us. First we must remove the mountains that block our creative thinking. Never reprogram and reinforce your mind with reasons that you can't be successful in fulfilling your purpose of service in life. "**All of us are born for a reason, but all of us don't discover why. Success in life has nothing to do with what you gain in life or accomplish for yourself. It's what you do for others."** Danny Thomas

Ask yourself questions and set your mind to seeking the answers. What special abilities has God already given me to uncover so that I can live a fulfilling and purposeful life? Robert Browning said, "**My business is not to make myself but make the absolute image of**

God." How can we become further connected with God to receive more creative thoughts?

Goals

"Happiness, wealth and success are by-products of goal-setting; they can not be the goal themselves."
                                                          John Condry

Goals are a *basis for motivation because they influence your performance and your tasks.* They direct your behavior and provide guidelines for how much effort you are willing to exert.

Actually, the more diffi-cult your goals, the higher level of performance you'll achieve. Commitment to a goal is proportional to its difficulty. Margaret Thatcher, who served as Prime Minister of Great Britain for 11 years becoming their longest serving this century, says,**"You may have to fight a battle more than once to win it."**

Also, the more specific the goal, the more concentrated the effort. We need that specific feedback to know how our efforts are doing. What are the quantitative and qualitative results you are trying to gain? **"There's a difference between interest and commitment. When you're interested in doing something, you do it only when it's convenient. When you're committed to something, you accept no excuses; only results."**
                                                          Kenneth Blanchard

To achieve our goals we must have motivation, which is addictive in the good sense, by the way. The only long-lasting motivation is *intrinsic*. Change jobs you are not interested in. Some 80% of the workers in the United States say they are unhappy doing their jobs. My favorite reply is, "Life is not a dress rehearsal."

Dorothea Brandt said, **"Don't concern yourself with how you're going to achieve your goals. Leave that to a power greater than yourself. All you need to know is where you are going and the answers will come to you."**

Our guidelines should be based on our values, ethics, and be in line with the legalities and policies of our world. What criteria have you set up so that you know you have achieved your goals? What resources are you asking the universe to give you in monetary and human form? Also, you need to keep in mind what are going to be the logical consequences of the achievement of your goals. What are the new opportunities for compensation, growth in discipline and knowledge, advancement, training, finances and development?

When you decide your goals, also decide which causes and concerns you want to support. Two things to consider: what are your personal concerns and what might be your customer's concerns? You might even choose a nonprofit organization if you checked out its integrity.

If you have been wondering why you didn't grow up to have goals like your brother and expect success, it is, of course, the way you were raised and educated. Males are taught that they are to master the situations that they encounter. They seek to be in control of their lives by overcoming fear, beating the odds, and being men of action. You, on the other hand, were not expected to take action or seek achievement. Girls might make good grades in school to please their parents rather than create stepping stones to further success. They were not expected to grow up self-reliant, independent, and responsible.

As children, girls are depicted in television and books as needing to be rescued, solving their problems by bursting into tears, or running off for help. Studies have shown that in school boys are called on more than girls. Even your mother met your brother's needs more quickly than yours! He was given more freedom to explore life while you were protected at home. In effect, you viewed the world as too dangerous and difficult. While Daddy was protecting you, the message was that you were not capable of handling your finances or decisions, much less your life!

Women have always served in the wars fought by our country, but it was not until 1975 that women were admitted to the U.S. Military Academy, the U.S. Naval Academy, the U.S. Air Force Academy, and the U.S. Coast Guard Academy. I met the mother of **Shannon Daughtery,** the young woman who has been trying for years to get into the Citadel. Her mother bought my books, *Life's Instruction Books for Women,* at a book signing. I wrote Shannon a special note of encouragement. Although the state tried to set up another school in South Carolina for Shannon to attend under the pretense that it will afford the same opportunities and teaching, her perserverance in her goals led ultimately to the decision that she could attend the Citadel thus advancing the fact that the school could no longer receive taxpayer money and not serve all the taxpayers?

Women must have the same opportunities growing up as males. If not, the same scenario will be repeated when they marry. And when the divorce comes or they are expected to make major decisions at work or in their business, they are not prepared to handle the stress of making all the decisions in life.

What are you to do? Get over it! First, recognize that you were born with the abilities and talents that will make you successful. You have the power to control your life and make correct decisions because you are able to think using your subconscious mind. **Determine your goals, write them down specifically, describe them with your sensory perceptions so that you can see and feel them.** You know that the only way your life is going to change and get better is when you start focusing on how you want your life to be. And to make your life change, you have to begin with yourself. **Change** is the key word here. Barbara Lyons reminds us, **"If we keep on doin' what we always done, we'll keep on gettin' what we always got."** When you start looking at your thoughts, ideas, activities and the information that comes to you with new awareness and consciousness, you become willing to expand and grow. I heard this concept called *"living on the skinny limbs"* because that is where the new growth occurs. **"Continuity gives us roots; change gives us branches, letting us stretch and grow and reach new heights."** Pauline Kezer

Second, focus on achieving your goals. Changing your self-image and perceptions of what you can do is a process that begins with a willingness to spend time to change your attitudes about yourself. Your self-esteem

"I realized that if what we call human nature can be changed, then absolutely anything is possible. And from that moment, my life changed."
                                                            Shirley McLaine

determines your ability to move into new areas with confidence. You need to feel capable of new knowledge and achievements.

Remember those girls who made you so mad because they always said they didn't do well on tests and then made an A.? Get over it, because they probably weren't very successful in life. Their problem? They had a split self-image which fluctuated from high to low. When things did not go well, their negative self-image confirmed that little else could be expected.

Actually, success, like everything else, is measured in degrees. When we get over "all or nothing" thinking, we realize that anything that we do has very little chance of being a total failure. Nellie Hershey Tullis notes, **"The next best thing to winning is losing! At least you've been in the race."** When we have reasonable expectations, we are able to succeed. **"The person who succeeds is not the one who holds back, fearing failure, or the one who never fails...but rather the one who moves on despite of failure."** Charles Swindell

The women who always talk about what they are going to do, but never take action, are avoiding the chance to fail. Gail Sheehy says, **"Changes are not only possible and predictable, but to deny them is to be an accomplice to one's own unnecessary vegetation."** The **excuse maker,** or the **procrastinator**, is always waiting for the right time or using other people as excuses why he can't take action. Really, the most unhappy people are the one who fear change the most. They fear losing the love of their friends or family. Some women work toward a goal or project, but never quite finish it. They lose interest because they fear the final product will not meet expectations. They fear making a mistake or being seen as a fool. Shirley Hufstedler says **"If you play it safe in life,** you've decided that you don't want to grow any more."

It's unrealistic to think that you aren't going to meet some rejection along the way. You have to have a plan for coping with rejection. You've got to expect a "no thanks" "or we've changed our mind" somewhere along the way. Many people decide that a rejection just gets them closer to an affirmative!

If you fear being criticized or breaking tradition and making changes, you will never take action. We get bogged down in the security of our habits and fear revealing who we really are. When someone asks you what you have been doing and your reply is the standard "nothing", this should tell you to get out of the rut. Lives are boring stuck in routine, repetition, and apathy with no challenges and opportunities.

There's a story about a frog who got stuck in a pothole in the road and couldn't get out. Various animals came along and tried to get him out, but couldn't. Feeling sorry for him, these animals decided to get him some food, but then the frog hopped past them. To their amazement, they asked the frog how he got out. His reply was, "a big tractor was coming along and I had to get out." Most of us have gotten used to sitting in the mud and refusing to do anything until we are forced to hop. Why wait? Elisabeth Kubler-Ross believes,

"We are solely responsible for our choices, and we have to accept the consequences for every deed, word and thought throughout our lifetime."

Goals

In contrast, some over-achievers take the joy out of success and over-works. Such a woman is compulsive about unimportant things, works harder, not smarter, and is critical of everyone else for not working as hard as she does. **"Happiness is in the taste and not in the things."**
La Rochefoucauld

Martina Navratilova, winner of nine Wimbleton championships and a record number of women's single titles advises us to, **"Just go out there and do what you've got to do."** You may not be as familiar with **"Babe" Didrikson Zaharis** but she is still considered by many to be the greatest woman athlete in the first half of the 20th century. At the 1932 Los Angeles Olympic games she won gold medals in the javelin throw and hurdles and tied for first in the high jump. Called the "Texas Tomboy," Babe won five gold medals at the Amateur Athletic Union championships. She helped found the Ladies Professional Golf Association and in 1955 wrote *This Life I've Led: My Autobiography.*

Self Esteem and Overcoming Fear

"An individual's self-concept is the core of his personality. It affects every aspect of human behavior: the ability to learn, the capacity to grow and change, the choice of friends, mates, and careers. It is no exaggeration to say that a strong, positive self-image is the best possible preparation for success in life."

Dr. Joyce Brothers

"No one can make you feel inferior without your consent."
" Remember always that you have not only the right to be an individual, you have an obligation to be one. You cannot make any useful contribution in life unless you do this." Eleanor Roosevelt

Your self-esteem influences all your actions and thereby your experiences. A spiritual woman knows to accept herself just as she is now. She doesn't see herself as perfect or superior to others because she is not in a comparative or competitive situation. Fanny Brice advised us, **"Let the world know you as you are, not as you think you should be-because sooner or later, if you are posing, you will forget the pose and then where are you?"** The spiritual woman has a strong sense of **consciousness, self-responsibility, assertiveness, integrity, purpose, and self-acceptance.** Her life is based on **total integrity** which means she doesn't back off from her principles, she **loves unconditionally and can recognize and apologize for her mistakes**. Her life is not ego-driven and she is interested in the other person's happiness. Because she is a unique creation and she possesses a sense of belonging to the cosmic universe, she knows that she must grow and change as the world and nature do. **"If we don't change, we don't grow. If we don't grow, we are not really living. Growth demands a temporary surrender of security."** Gail Sheehy As a result, a spiritual woman greets new challenges with all her energies. She knows that as she unfolds her true self, her heightened awareness in the world will grow richer and more rewarding. It has been said that fear gives intelligence even to fools. One of my greatest fears would be to live a life of boredom. **"Millions long for immortality who don't know what to do on a rainy afternoon."** Susan Ertz

Harriet Quimby who lived from 1875-1912 was the first licensed American woman pilot. She was also the first woman authorized to carry the U.S. mail. Think of what fears she must have overcome to fly across the English Channel. The next year **Georgia (Tiny) Broadwick** became the first American woman to parachute from an airplane.

A lot of fish grow in direct proportion to the size of the water in which they live. In the same respect, **people grow in proportion to the size of their world.** It's not the physical world but the spiritual, mental and emotional opportunities to which we open ourselves. Growth comes from the inside to the outside. **"What you become is far more important than what you get. What you get will be influenced by what you become."** Jim Rohn

Previous thinking about success and changing our behaviors said that if only we had more will power, we could change our self-esteem and all that ails us. Dr. Maxwell Maltz said, **"We act, or fail to act, not because of 'will' as is so commonly believed, but because of imagination."** He also added about our embracing life, **"You are embarking on the greatest adventure of your life, to improve your self-image, to create more meaning in your life and in the lives of others."**

We are to use a synthetic imagination that combines facts, concepts, ideas, or plans in a new way. Then we use our creative imagination to make these new thoughts reflect our commitment and purpose. Now we know that we must change our belief systems about who we really are. We form a creative vision that overcomes our imposed limitations, handicaps, and opposing forces. Paula P. Brownlee notes, **"To do good things in the world, first you must know who you are and what gives meaning in your life."** We perform consistently in a manner the way we see ourselves. That is, we act in a direct proportion to our direct image. **"You are not what I think you are, you are not what you think you are, you are what you think I think you are."** Rev. Robert Schuller We must first change our inward perceptions in order to change our outer actions.

"If you want to be a winner," says Denis Waitley, **"Winning is a reflex action. If you've been there in your mind, you'll go there in your body."** Most women utilize these favorable qualities without thinking that those are the basis of who they really are and that they can enhance their lives further by demonstrating them more. **"The more self-awareness a person has the more alive he is."** Rollo May

For example, most women demonstrate power when they survive a divorce which sends them out into the work force, making them solely responsible for the home and yard and acting as primary caretakers for the children. I call this **POWER!** And yet, women have huge amounts of untapped power; they need to overcome negative emotions associated with divorce (anger and revenge) unfettering the controls of an ex-husband, and overcoming guilt in dealing with their children. When a mother demonstrates a lack of power, the children grow up not feeling safe. Studies about children of divorce show that many times they either take longer or never develop their full potential.

Jessica McClintock has survived being a widow and being divorced. She has one child and is the CEO of Jessica McClintock., a company that sells perfume, bridal dresses, and dresses in addition to bed-and-bath products. By the end of 1995 she will have expanded to the casual-apparel market and will have 22 specialty boutique shops this year alone.. Sales are now at $149 million.

Power has been redefined to mean "**the capacity to implement.**" The connotation of the word means to control or limit others. Madeleine Kunin emphasizes, **"Women need to see ourselves as individuals capable of creating change. That is what political and economic power is all about: having a voice, being able to shape the future. Women's absence from decision-making positions has deprived the country of a necessary perspective."** We can have power in our lives without taking away another's power. Our aim should be the development of fulfilling individual lives. We have inherent abilities which give us power. As we develop our power, our goal is not to advance over others, but to advance our inner perceptions.

Power is sttrength and the ability to see yourself through your own eyes and not through the eyes of another. It is being able to place a circle of power at you own feet and not take power from someone else's circle.   Lynn V. Andrews

---

Dr. Laura Schlessinger, author of *Ten Stupid Things Women Do To Mess Up Their Lives,* is one of the most powerful women I have heard speak. She has a nationally syndicated radio talk show, where women call in for advice. Her main advice directs women to be **responsible** for their own lives and not give away their **power** for self-determination to their mate. She definitely does not believe women should continue their "victim" philosophy. Dr. Schlessinger feels that women do not concentrate on their own lives and agendas and consequently make mistakes which trap them into unproductive lives.

Betty Friedan published in 1981, *The Second Stage,* in which she called for equality between women and men in all phases of life. Friedan criticized the women's movement because of its negativeness, especially in family relationships.

The focus of power should be to seek lives of effectiveness. When you are living in the present moment, past attitudes of power are no longer pertinent. A principle centered life will seek all the resources necessary. **"Research on the links between achievement, motivation and self-image suggests that possible selves, future selves, are part of one's self-image and are keys to success or failure."** Hazel Markus

Success Through Spirituality For Women

Barbara Jordon, former congresswoman from Texas is one of the most powerful women in America. She said of herself, **"I never intended to become a run-of-the-mill person."** She made a keynote speech to the Democratic National Convention, the first given at a major party's national convention. She won wide notice for her keen questioning during the televised House Judicary Committee hearings on the proposed impeachment of Richard Nixon. She said, **"Do not call for black power or green power. Call for brain power."** Women are said to try to get power by charming or nagging, but Jordon proclaims an authentic voice of power demonstrated by her unswerving confidence in her beliefs.

Women don't need to use sexual signals to gain power nor do they need to scream, throw tantrums, flatter, threaten, whine, shock, or pressure people. They don't need to play men's games about positioning in a room, tactical positions, or word play. Power comes from knowing that you know what is right and you have the insight into how to achieve it. When you argue with someone, that person drains your energy. **"If women understood and exercised their power they could remake the world."** Emily Taft Douglas

Janice Parsons turned her family's antique business into Bead Happy. At her shop customers can assemble their own jewelry as well as buy beads already made into necklaces, earrings, bracelets, etc. Those who want training on how to make several items with beads can sign up for classes at Bead University. Parson believes," ...**beads are empowering and then, through creativity, people can increase their self-esteem."** Bead Happy brought in sales over $1 million in 1993 and is still growing.

71

Self Esteem and Overcoming Fear

My friend who recently graduated as a paralegal was discussing job opportunities with a counselor. She felt a ball on the end of her tongue which prevented her from speaking positively about herself which she knew she would have to do to obtain a job.

The external facts told her that she had graduated from the class, but her internal representations of herself told her she was not smart because somewhere in her past someone told her she wasn't. Her solution, according to *NLP (Neuro Linguistic Programming, The New Technology of Achievement),* is to change her image of herself by picturing herself in mind as a bright and creative woman. This woman possesses intuitive feeling, and at times is so sensitive to others' feelings she picks up their negative energies. With this quality, she needs to be in the people business rather than behind a computer. She has a keen interest in how the colors we wear and those around us affect us, but she has not taken a chance on herself to market her knowledge.

The next book on your reading list should be *NLP, The New Technology of Achievement,* edited by **Steve Andreas** and **Charles Faulner**. Don't let the title scare or put you off. This is a life-changing book because it teaches you ways to control your mind by focusing on the facts, ideas, and impressions that you want to think about. The techniques free your mind of negative, destructive thinking and encourage positive, inner thinking. The book does not relate directly to spirituality, but we are aware that God has given us minds capable of unlimited learning and growth and this book tells us how to do it.

When we can overcome **a fear of being evaluated or being judged** and **then found lacking,** then we overcome the fear of failure. Susan Anthony said, **"Cautious, careful people, always casting about to preserve their** reputations...can never affect a reform." Unfortunately, there are those who do achieve success and then worry that they will be expected to continue achievement. They start then to self-sabotage their own success. Whether it is by nature or through learned behavior, females tend to fear failure more than males. The non-competitive games we played as children did not teach us how to handle failure. And if that isn't bad enough, we females have a harder time bouncing back from failure. We do not take the attitude of **failure as a learning experience,** plus we then become doubters about our future successes. We confuse failure of our actions with failure of ourselves! Marlo Thomas advises, **"One of the things about equality is not just that you be treated equally to a man, but that you treat yourself equally to the way you treat a man."**

Maryt Wollstonecraft says, **"I do not wish women to have power over men, but over themselves."**

Here are some role models of women who took action to achieve their goals:

Ernesta Procope, called the First Lady of Wall Street for 40 years, became successful as a minority woman in a traditionally male establishment. She founded E.G. Bowman Co. Inc., an insurance brokerage firm, which had $35 million in premiums last year. Think of this lady when you fear unconventional professions and prejudice and remember what she had to overcome.

Henrietta Howland Robinson was an American financier who lived from 1834-1916 who turned a $1 million inheritance into $100 million. Hetty Green, as she was known, was called the "witch of Wall Street" because of her eccentricities. Marlo Thomas has noted that, **"A man has to be Joe McCarthy to be called ruthless. All a woman has to do is put you on hold."**

Self Esteem and Overcoming Fear

Loida N. Lewis took over TLC Beatrice when her husband, legendary African-American corporate deal-maker Reginald Lewis, passed away. She observed a year of mourning before she took over the business in 1994. Now she is in control of a multi-national grocery business. TLC Beatrice has sales of $1.82 billion making her the top women's business owner in America. She's somebody who makes decisions people can respect.

Akey Creech had to radically change her belief system in 1990. She runs a livestock feeding and manufacturing company doing sales of $120 million with 250 employees. She purchased the company from her father in 1988. Then in 1990 she had a religious conversion which changed her life. She described herself as being an alcoholic prior to that. Now she runs her business on Christian principles such as a company policy which disallows alcohol on expense reports and at company events. This policy has not hurt the company which reported a 6% growth last year.

Pleasant Rowland started the Pleasant Company in 1986 because she was frustrated that Barbie was the role model for young girls. Rowland, a former teacher, text book author, and television news anchor, began with $1 million royalties she made with her books, the American Girls Collection. A trip to Williamsburg was her inspiration for the series. She also publishes **American Girl Magazine** which has 450,000 subscribers. The company has expanded and sells girls clothing in its catalogs. Sales last year were $152 million.

Risk-taker, **Margaret Sanger** published a 16-page pamphlet called, **Family Limitation**, which defied government bans on dissemination of birth-control information. **Woman Rebel**, was a magazine founded by

Sanger which carried articles on contraception. William Sanger, her husband, was put on trial because he carried a copy of the pamphlet. He was convicted and sent to serve 30 days in jail.

History proves two things: a country that does not allow freedom of expression, rights, and individual thinking will never be economically powerful and secondly, a country which discriminates and keeps part of its citizens repressed is repressing itself. **Rosalyn Yalow**, nuclear physicist and Nobel Prize winner for medicine in 1977 said,

> "The World cannot afford the loss of the talents of half its people if we are to solve the many problems which beset us."

Selected Readings
Sanford, Linda T., and Mary Ellen Donovan, *Women and Self-esteem: Understanding and Improving the Way We think and Feel About Ourselves.* New York: Doublday, Naomi Wolf, **Fire with Fire: The New Female Power and How It Will Change the 21st Century**
This book is better and more important than **The Beauty Myth: How Images of Beauty Are Used Against Women, Naomi** Wolf, New York: Anchor Books, 1992, because it calls for feminism to re-connect its power base to all women who are interested in equal rights. Separate ideas on pornography, sexuality, abortion, and political affiliation may differ, but women need to unite in their need for knowing how economic and political strides can be made.

Using Your God Given Resources

BRAINS

"There is a growing strength in women, but it's in the forehead, not in the forearm."
Beverly Sills

I've always believed that **we don't work our brains because we don't know how our brains work.** We may have learned what to call the various parts of the brain and how they were responsible for the functions of our bodies, but little or no time was spent on how to utilize the power of our brains and how to access knowledge through our connection with the universe.

Educators and motivators have compared the brain to a computer saying that it takes in information. We now know that our brains are able to do significantly more when we learn to think quantum rather than linear.

"How many women are ready to admit that they are capable of changing the course of their existence by simply taking time to think? It is easy for them to persuade themselves that the future, luck, chance, and the stars too, are the matters of their fortune. Is it their fault? For centuries fatalism has been passed on to all babies wearing pink booties even as they lie in their bassinets."
Christiane Collange

Facts You Should Know About Your Brain

- Your brain is in a constant state of change because it responds to what you think and to your experiences.
- In a **split second** your brain can compute and relay responses. It only takes 200 milli-seconds for your eyes and brain to communicate.
- Brains need to be exercised and freed from mental stress to work at peak performance.
- Though you lose your brain cells as you grow older, you still have five million to work with. So while you might lose some of your long-term memory, your brain is still growing and you have an amazing ability to keep learning. It is probably a blessing because **we need to live in the present anyway.**
- Give your brain problems to sort, perceive, and analyze. Do you know that when your brain goes into action, neurotransmitters go into high gear, capillaries expand, and your blood flow increases which then increases your oxygen and decreases your carbon dioxide?
- Alcohol shrinks and kills the brain's neurons.
- Exercise that is continuous and rhythmic and gets your heartbeat up is good for the brain.
- When creativity or **mindfulness** becomes such a vital part of your thinking, you will not only probably live longer, but will transform you into your true self.
- We are all born with creativity and our minds' desire to grow.
- A Canadian neurosurgeon discovered that when a person is forced to change a fundamental belief or opinion, the brain undergoes a series of nervous sensations equivalent to distressing torture. **Neuro Linguistic Programming** can show you how to easily make those

changes. It is our approach to change that needs to change. Since change is inevitable, you can go with the flow or be coerced.

■ Learning Strategies Corporation in Wayzata, Minnesota, has created the PhotoReading Whole Mind System which you read by photographing the entire page with your subconscious mind. Later, you activate to gain comprehension. The system teaches you to instruct your subconscious mind to look for just the material you need. You are taught to relax, become aware, and then to search out pertinent information by quickly going through the material's whole pages at once.

■ **The Journal of Neuroscience** says men's brains are 10% larger than women's, but women's brains are more densely packed with neurons. This means that our brain cells are squeezed into a smaller space. The researchers say that men and women aren't wired the same which accounts for why we act differently.

Dr. Sandra Witelson, the study's leading author, says that the tighter density in the cerebral cortex of the temporal lobe, a region used for "higher intellectual activities," had never been seen in human brains before. They found that the "isthmus" part of the corpus collosum is now known to be bigger in women than in men. The isthmus connects the two hemispheres of the corpus collosum and is packed with nerve fibers used in communication. This gives credence to the thought that women have better communication and verbal skills than men.

A perfect example of women's abilities is **Mae Jemison** who is a medical doctor, chemical engineer, and scientist. She can speak Swahili, Russian, and Japanese and still finds time to be a serious dancer and have a cameo appearance on *Star Trek: The Next Generation.*

Her concern in life is West Africa's health care and an international science camp for youths.

Ritchie Barthello believes that the computer age has accelerated brain activity. I agree because it takes the drudgery out of writing and allows much more creativity. Ritchie and **Andrea Barthello** started a company in 1985 that designs, manufactures, and sells brain teaser puzzles because Ritchie loves puzzles. Their company, Binary Arts sells to stores such as Natural Wonders and Imaginarium. Sales are at $5 million.

Doug Hall and David Wecker wrote *Jump Start Your Brain*, a book that reveals how you can retrain your brain to think more creatively. Hall, a toy inventor, tells stories of his experiences with such companies as Nike, AT&T, and Disney.

Studies show that our brains are affected in a predictable way by certain odors. The odors that travel to the nose dissolve in the moisture of nasal tissue. Olfactory cells pass on the smells to the hypothalamus in the brain. This organ regulates temperature, hunger, blood sugar levels, sleep, sexual desires, growth, wakefulness, and emotions such as anger and happiness. Our memories of smells are stored in the hippocampus, located in the brain.

AromaSys is a four-year-old company located in Minneapolis that studies the psychological and physiological effects of aroma. Aromas can make you alert, relaxed, sleepy, or refreshed. The company is busy creating new patents of smells. The Japanese are checking out office aromatherapy.

Company owners need to be aware that sound, stress, meals, and work schedules affect employees. **Pierce Howard**, author of *The Owner's Manual for the Brain,* says that brain research should be applied to many business problems. Shift workers who have to change their hours often suffer depression from changing sleep habits. The amount of sleep we need varies, but our brains are set on a 25-hour day rather than 24 and they needs at least 90 minutes of uninterrupted sleep to work productively the next day. Actually, we do the exact wrong thing when we don't get enough sleep and then we drink extra coffee or Coke adding caffeine to our system. Caffeine is a stimulant that releases the brain chemical cortisol, which increases our stress levels. You might be more alert, but your brain will not be able to make good judgments. If you dream while getting a good night's sleep, you'll have an improved brain the next day. To be successful, you need to feel your best so learn to relax your brain and your body before trying to go to sleep.

"You are the product of your own brainstorm."
Rosemary Konner Steinbaum

Emotions

We are under the false impressions that our emotions control us. Actually, if we don't control our emotions, especially our negative emotions, they will be detrimental to our success. **"A life of reaction is a life of slavery, intellectually and spiritually. One must fight for a life of action, not reaction."** Rita Mae Brown We can only think of one thing at a time, so our emotions are giving us thoughts of fear, anger, or anxiety and our thinking will actually be slowed down. **"You gain strength, courage and confidence by every experience in which you really stop to look fear in the face. You are able to say to yourself, 'I lived through this horror. I can take the next thing that comes along. You must do the thing you think you cannot do.'"** Eleanor Roosevelt You won't fail if you don't try, but who wants to live this way? **"It is no sin to attempt and fail. The only sin is not to make the attempt."** SuEllen Fried

"We need time to dream, time to remember, and time to reach the infinite. Time to be."
Gladys Taber

"Creativity is especially expresssing the ability to make connections to make associations, to turn things around and express them in a new way," says Tim Hansen. When I am expanding my mind and am thinking creatively, the energy in my brain goes wild. My speech gets faster and more animated, reflecting the explosion of electrical activity going on. Creativity is

81

heightened and more connections and decisions are made. Mary Lou Cook says, **"Creativity is inventing, experimenting, growing, taking risks, breaking rules, making mistakes, and having fun."** We are able to be more innovative and solve problems with creative solutions. **Creative people all have one thing in common, they think they are creative. It's their attitude.**

Dreams

"A dream is an ideal involving a sense of possibilities rather than probabilities, of potential rather than limits. A dream is the wellspring of passion, giving us direction and pointing us to lofty heights. It is an expression of optimism, hope and values lofty enough to capture the imagination and engage the spirit. Dreams grab us and move us. They are capable of lifting us to new heights and overcoming self-imposed limitations."
Robert Kriegel

"The future belong to those who believe in the beauty of their dreams. " Eleanor Roosevelt

When we say dreams we may be referring to hopes for the future or the pictures that occur while you sleep. Both types are helpful in creating success.

Do you know that you can increase your brainpower by paying attention to the illusions and allusions going on when you dream? You can even train yourself to remember your dreams. It's a good idea to record your dreams on paper. And then if you take time to study your dreams, you'll get more out of them.

Dreams work with the body's energy and they have value. You are the producer of your own dreams so you are the best person to interpret them. You may even need to dream to get rid of excessive thought overload. Or you may choose to dream to get the answer to a question or problem. I have received my most creative marketing ideas and solutions to problems this way. The more you choose to dream, the more suggestions will come to you. *Creative Dreaming*, by **Patricia Garfield** will teach you how to remember your dreams.

Precognitive dreams are psychic visions and give you information about the future through symbols. When you have a **lucid dream** you are aware that you are dreaming. Then you have the ability to control your dreams. You can use this time to visualize the way you want to be in life, and resolve questions. You can interpret your dreams using your other psychic abilities. We've all sensed a feeling of d'eja vu when we think we have already seen something. And if you think you have forgotten what you dreamed, you can shift to your psychic vision area and see it again and alert your other psychic senses to help you. It would be worthwhile to spend time learning how to dream and interpret your dreams.

The other kind of dream, your hope for the future is equally important. If you don't have a dream, how are you going to know where you are going? Sheila Murray Bethel said in, *Making a Difference*, **"One of the most courageous things you can do is identify yourself, know who you are, what you believe in, and where you want to go."** We make the mistake of either not having a dream, giving up on it too soon, or letting them lie dormant. Or we have small dreams to protect ourselves from failure.

"The most pathetic person in the world is someone who has sight, but has no vision." Helen Keller

"There are people who put their dreams in a little box and say, "Yes, I've got dreams, of course, I've got dreams" Then they put the box away and bring it out once in a while to look in it, and yep, they're still there. These are great dreams, but they never even get out of the box. It take an uncommon amount of guts to put your dreams on the line, to hold them up and say, "How good or how bad am I?" That's where courage comes in." Erma Bombeck

"What a man is, is the basis of what he dreams and thinks, accepts and rejects, feels and perceives." John Mason Brown To be successful, you must fantasize and dream constantly about how to achieve your goals and then act on them on a day-to-day basis. Dream about what is possible and write them down. Creative imagination is built by dreaming. Walt Disney said, "All our dreams can come true- if we have the courage to pursue them."

Mark Juarez started Tender Loving Things out of a desire to help people worldwide. One night he dreamed about creating a Happy Massager, a wooden ball with legs and arms. It massages acupressure points. He now sells $10.6 million dollars a years in America and Japan and hopes to break into other markets.

Former First Lady, Rosalyn Carter wrote, " If we have not achieved our early dreams we must either find new ones or see what we can salvage from the old. If we have accomplished what we set out to do in youth, then we need not weep like Alexander the Great that we

have no more worlds to conquer. There is clearly much left to be done, and whatever else we are going to do, we had better get on with it."

Sleep

Our minds have the ability to take our thoughts and allow them to form, develop and "pop up" in our unconscious and subconscious levels. We awaken at night knowing that our minds have been actively working on our problems, decisions, and activities. I compose most of my letters and the summaries of masses of materials while I am sleeping. When I record my new insights, problem solving, or writings immediately after awakening, they are exactly the information I want to convey arranged in logical sequence and clarity. Anytime you use your *conscious mind,* your subconscious mind is put to sleep to allow you to innovate inspired thinking.

Memory

Our memories should serve us rather than destroy us. If we seek to remember failures, pains, regrets, and bad memories, we lack fulfillment. Our past unhappiness or failures should only be remembered to enable us to make corrections in our lives. This is the way we learn and mature.

We've known things all our lives, but when we can understand those things in a new way, we are learning.

Choose to remember your good qualities, talents, and strengths. You can train your mind to use correct thinking. Then you have a clear picture of the purpose and meaning of the activities in your life. Stress and problems are not new to our lives. As a matter of fact, we are offered a wider choice of solutions today. **When our minds are inspired and thinking creatively, there is no room in our lives for things which have no value, no constructive purpose or higher thinking.**

Think back over a day you wasted "stewing" over a problem, relationship, or situation trying to find answers in your mind. The *true* answer was already established and waiting for you to seek it. Your soul has an accumulated wisdom- divine laws, principles and archetypes. We are not the unworthy weaklings that we are encouraged to think we are! **God has given us a conscious mind, soul directed, to become totally alive and complete.**

To be successful, you must use all the resources you have. Improving your memory will help you remember names and people, when you give presentations you will remember facts, figures and prices, and you will test better. Listen to **Kevin Trudeau's** Mega Memory tape which teaches that we remember everything through pictures, not concepts, words, or ideas. **We think in pictures.** Trudeau said that he read everything he could about memory because he was a failing student. He teaches that instead of spending time writing down information we want to remember, we should picture it in our mind. You must put information in our memories in the form of pictures. The neurotransmitter is stimulated. You reach a level of unconscious competence.

When I think of how I spell words it is not through their sounds but how I picture the word in my mind. We are actually releasing our instant recall memory. How many of us think that we are not smart because we can not remember facts, dates, names, or figures? Learn to chain or link in your mind's eye information through pictures vividly using all your senses. *Pychocybernetics,* by **Maxwell Maltz**, states that the body does not know the difference between that which is real and that which is vividly imagined. If you are home alone at night and hear an unusual noise, you can become terrified thinking that a burglar is in your house when it may be the wind blowing a branch on your window.

To remember something, you shift your thinking to the area called the **"third eye"** or focal center which is located above your eyebrows in the middle of your forehead. The **"third eye"** is the way we see psychic vision. An abstract picture in the form of a color pattern or maybe a figure appears. You should pay attention when you receive these images. As you experience life you store visual images of the events, people and places. Your memory takes in everything that is going on every moment of your life. We have a choice about what we want to focus on.

Pegging, Trudeau says, is a conscious applied memory technique that establishes mental places where we can store memory. Later when you want to recall the information, you know where to go.

Problems

If you want to do all you can do, take on more than you think is possible. After all, all development is self-development.

"Many intelligent adults are restrained in thoughts, actions, and results. They never move further than the boundaries of their self-imposed limitation."
John C. Maxwell

Gail Sheehy in her book, *New Passages: Mapping Your Life Across Time*, talks about how much has changed since she wrote *Passages* in 1976. As a 50 year-old, I can relate to the sentiments expressed by others that age in the book. When I was young I never thought I'd be 50 or even know anyone that old. Now 50 is like being 40. Every age seems to be moved back. On one hand, children seem to be maturing so much younger than they did, but people in their 30's seem to act so much younger.

The good news Sheehy gives us is that if a woman reaches 50 free of cancer and heart disease, she can expect to live until 92. My grandmother died at 92 so when I decided to start a new career at 49, I was looking to be alive 43 more years! Instead of 50 being considered old, *Passages* suggests that it is a time of second adulthood that offers new possibilities.

Sheehy says that men are not as optimistic about the future as women and that they are tired and "running out of gas." Since most women have been caretakers until about 40, many begin to bloom when they decide what they want to do. The book suggests that you find your passion. Over 1 million women over 40 are using their time to go back to school. Contrary to what most people think, only 10 of Americans 65 and over have chronic health problems.

Sheehy notes, *"In the hundreds of interviews I have done with men and women in middle life...people are beginning to see there is the exciting potential of a new life to live: one in which they can concentrate on becoming better, stronger, deeper, wiser, funnier, freer, sexier and more attentive to living the privileged moments."* No matter what age you are, I would suggest that you read **New Passages**.

The two poorest groups in the US. today are women raising children alone and women over 65 living alone. The number of households headed by a single woman increased to 21 percent in 1990. Nearly half of all single-mother households were below the poverty line in 1991. The purpose of this book is to offer preventive measures and solutions so that you do not fall into either of these two groups.

If you think that you are going to be able to live on your Social Security, you are living in a dream world. Only 10% of women receive any benefits at all from private pension plans. Of full-time workers, only 46% are covered by private pension plans, including 43% of full -time working women and 50% of men. The average annual pension for women over 65 was $5,220 in 1989, compared to $8,649 for men.

Only 13% of workers earning less than $10,000 annually have benefits that include a pension plan, and only 41% of those earning between $10,000 and $20,000 have one. This should be of special importance to women since 2/3 of working women earned less than $20,000 in 1988.

In businesses with 100 or fewer employees, only 24% have pension coverage, yet 45% of working women are employed by such companies. Women also make up more than 2/3 of all part-time employees, concentrated mostly on lower-paying occupations, and these jobs, too, can be excluded from pension plans. The government reports that in 1991 18.3 million people were making money in home-based businesses, 65% of them women.

A report from the U.S. Department of Labor, Women's Bureau, says traditionally, women have "crowded" into a few occupations. In 1989 the six most prevalent occupations for women were, in order of magnitude, secretaries, school teachers (excluding those teaching in colleges and universities), semi-skilled machine operators, managers and administrators, retail and personal sales workers, and bookkeepers and accounting clerks. In 1989 about one-third of all women at work were employed in these occupations. It has been argued that women choose these occupations because there tends to be less skill obsolescence for workers who leave and reenter the labor force. It has also been argued that the educational commitment for employment in these fields is less than in some others, and workers can have more time at home for other responsibilities.

To earn more money than they are in the non-skilled work they are now doing, women need to train in skilled trades where they now only represent 8.7 of the workers. Women represent 26% of the manual workers-operators, fabricators, and laborers. In 1988 only two percent of all employed women were in the skilled labor trade- precision production, craft, and repair occupations. In these areas women receive approximately equal, or even greater compensation than their male coworkers in the same occupations. In the more traditional jobs, such as teachers or nurses, employers with large numbers of employees can still act to keep wages low (monopsony), and this strategy coupled with the fewer hours worked by women than men tend to keep weekly and annual earnings of all women well below those of all men.

Women seeking skilled jobs should try to get into apprenticeship programs which are commonly registered with the Federal Government or a federally approved State apprenticeship agency. Registered programs offer apprenticeships in over 800 occupations such as carpenter, plumber, aircraft mechanic (electrical and radio), tool and die maker, T.V. and radio repair, and others. Apprentices who successfully complete registered programs receive certificates of completion from the U.S. Department of Labor or a federally approved state apprenticeship agency. Most registered programs are sponsored jointly by employers and labor unions. The administrative body in such joint programs is called a Joint Apprenticeship Committee (JAC). Currently, there are approximately 44,000 program sponsors and more than 300,000 registered apprentices.

Fortunes have been made the last few years in the field of computer science, and yet women make up less than 10% of the industry. When women stop choosing to sell the cutesy, the unnecessary, and the low cost merchandise and begin selling the basics of business and finance, they will earn more money and find their niche.

The pink-collar workers, telephone operators, secretaries, data processors, and clerks make up the largest occupational group, and are very likely to suffer heart disease because they are the least in control of their lives or work for bosses who have coronary heart disease.

Problems

Look at the office environment your company provides for you to know how much they are concerned for your emotional well-being and self-esteem. Most offices that I have visited that are not trying to impress affluent clients are painted beige or off-white, with no pictures, plants, or visual diversions. The monotony of working in catacomb cubicles in front of a computer lowers self-esteem and promotes stress.

Working Woman Magazine did an article about women who work at a Nabisco Foods plant in Oxnard, California. The workers spent tedious hours on their feet to process, pack, and label food products. They were only allowed three breaks during the day, for seven minutes each, where 200 women were supposed to use 12 toilets. Men working for the company were not subject to the same rules. The company said that because of the type of job, workers had to raise their hand for a relief worker, who rarely seemed to appear.

Fortunately, employees are getting smarter about their rights. New sexual harassment laws or enforcing the current ones, acts such as the Americans With Disabilities and the Civil Rights Act, are making companies more responsive to labor disagreements. Reports of sexual discrimination and sexual harassment increased dramatically in the 1980's. Women were more likely than men to lose their jobs or get their wages cut then, too. In the '90's women make up more that 60% of the personnel and labor-relations managers. Women still have a long way to go to get equity in the court systems. This is a field where you can easily combine your purpose in life in helping others.

To know the truth about how our media manipulates statistics and presents false information about women's status in American, I would suggest that you read

Backlash by Susan Faludi. She talks about the false reports of "the man shortage scares" and "the infertility scare". Women need only to listen to the radio to know about the decline in respect for women and then read the newspaper to know about the increase in sexual violence. Knowing the truth about our status should not be defeating but should strengthen our resolve to be stronger. You have already witnessed the discrimination of **Christine Kraft, Kathleen Sullivan, Jane Pauley,** and **Connie Chung** on television. It took until 1976 for **Barbara Walters** to become the first woman co-anchor on an American network evening news program. House Speaker **Newt Gingrich's** mother nationally criticized Connie Chung when she said Chung made her say bad things about the First Lady, **Hillary Rodham Clinton**. We must take **personal responsibility** for our words and our actions. **No one can make us say things!**

To achieve spiritual success, you must stand up for your beliefs, live a principled life, and be strong enough to stand against those who try take away your power through sexual harassment. All women for all times have had to endure sexual harassment, but it doesn't have to continue. You must have power in all the areas of your life: financial, emotional, and social so that when you are approached, you are first aware of the harassment, then intolerant of it, and then know how to protect yourself. Congress can pass the laws, but women must be willing to document, report, and stand powerfully. We must support each other and quit blaming ourselves. Take time to read our women's history and model the strong women who stood up for their rights.

Mike Tyson was recently released from prison for raping a young black woman. A well-planned media event to promote his next fight was held in Harlem, New

Problems

York but was strongly protested by blacks who said that no matter how much money a person has or what his position is, too many young black women are being sexually assaulted. The turnout in support of Tyson was small. Strangely enough, the strong Tyson entered and left with a slew of body guards encircling him. He has never been apologetic for his actions.

Divorce is considered the second most devastating event in a person's life after the death of a spouse. Many women have found that divorce can be an important springboard that inspires them to change in ways that they did not know were possible. *"When one door of happiness closes, another opens; but often we look so long at the closed door that we do not see the one which has been opened for us."* Helen Keller Here are truths women found about themselves after their divorce:

(1)   Over 80% of women experience a new sense of independence and strength to survive.

(2)   80% have a more positive self-image and higher self- esteem.

(3)   Seeking female friends bolsters self esteem.

(4)   Divorce forces women to come to terms with their own identities.

(5)   Women adapt and change in response to the obstacles which they encounter.

(6)   Many women find that they are happier than they have ever been.

(7)   Divorce allows women to do the things which they never had the opportunity to do being married, such as going back to school or seeking a new career.

(8)   Most women become more confident as they experience new feelings of accomplishment as they stand alone.

(9)   Women can choose to go back into the role of
         being co-dependent or they can make the decision
         to be proactive, taking responsibility for their lives.

The attitude about battered wives has changed so it is no longer considered a domestic issue. Intimate crimes are no longer private issues. Batterers are now being taken to task for their crimes by more extensive prosecution and conviction. The **Violence Against Women Program Office** makes sure grants are properly distributed. Bonnie Campbell heads the agency which controls the $800 million dollar budget. The YWCA is sponsoring **Week Without Violence**, starting October 15. The National Coalition for Domestic Volence is creating a national registry of victims called, **Remember My Name Memorial.**

Black professional women outnumber black professional men almost 2 to 1 in corporate America according to the US. Equal Employment Opportunity Commission. The Wall Street Journal did a study which found that black professional women have made a 125% increase between 1982 and 1992. They fall behind black men in the areas of officers and managers though they have increased their numbers. Just as white women do not make as much as white men in most areas, black women make 14% less than black men. A larger percentage of black women work compared to white and Hispanic, but the numbers are changing.

Many people use the lack of a college education as an excuse for not trying to be successful. Marta and Steve Weinstein co-founded a $200 million firm, Logistix, providing manufacturing, assembly, and packaging services to businesses like Apple, Hewlett Packard, and Adobe. The Weinteins had no strategic plan nor any particular technical expertise. They called themselves the "miracle mix" because without one another the business would have failed.

We all know that **Albert Einstein** was not considered smart in high school, and that his Ph.D. dissertation was rejected at the University of Bern in 1905 because professors said it was irrelevant and fanciful.

"There is no meaning to life except the meaning man gives his life by the unfolding of his powers. To 'maximize our potential' we must take advantage of the resources available designed to increase our understanding of ourselves, the people around us, and the life we are now involved in. We become what we indulge ourselves in. The opportunities life offers help us tap our potential and can be explored when we are equipped with the right tools."

Erich Fromm

Mary Crowley, successful businessperson and author, says, **"We are who we are today because of the choices we made yesterday. Likewise, tomorrow will become the result of today's choices. We are free up to the point of choice, then the choice controls the chooser."**

Your past does not have to foretell your future or your potential. What is true in your life now is not what has to be in the future. You are a successful woman waiting to emerge! It has been said, **"The undeveloped piece of property with the greatest potential is still between the ears."** We know that all people are not given the same abilities, but we have *the equal ability to become unequal.*

Benjamin Barber notes that there are two types of people in the world. *"There are people who learn, who are open to what happens around them, who listen, who hear the lessons. When they do something stupid, they don't do it again. And when they do something that*

96

works a little bit, they do it even better and harder the next time. The question to ask is not whether you are a success or failure, but whether you are a learner or a nonlearner."

> Do you know that finance is a good place for women to excel because there is little or no wage discrimination. More that half of U.S. accountants are women.

Most of the women who run companies doing millions in sales inherited their businesses. They had to continue to learn to keep them successful and increase profits. **Nanci Mackenzie**, the President of U.S. Gas Transportation with sales of $130 million and 17 employees, started the company. She started working for a fuel-oil broker in the 60's to support her children . On the side she sold diesel fuel for another company which gave her the cash to later buy half of her employer's business. Later she started Lucky Lady Oil. Nanci Mackenzie graduated from Southern State Teachers College which probably did not offer her courses in business and marketing. Like most of us, she had to rely on her knowledge and skills to run her business.

In 1985 **Kavelle Bajay** began her computer net-working company called I-Net. Being a woman and a minority, she faced many obstacles. Through her hard work and desire to succeed, I-Net was successful. Sales are over $230 million this year with over 2,570 employees.

"Some people make victims of their disadvantages, while others are victimized by their disadvantages."

Robert Schuller

Problems

The next time you whine about your problems, consider **Donna Conner** who played backup center for the Monmouth College basketball team with a 61.9% accuracy. She averaged 19 points and 15 rebounds in high school, scoring 1,604 points. But she can't drive a car or read a magazine because Donna was born with 20/300 vision in one eye and 20/400 vision in the other eye.

Olympic gold-medal winner, Joan Benoit, underwent knee surgery only 17 days before the US. Olympic trials. She made the trials and later became a winner in the marathon.

"Problems are not stops signs, they are guidelines."
Robert Schuller

How many of us would have considered an acting career if we were deaf? **Marlee Matlin**, who starred in *Children of a Lesser God,* won an Academy Award for best actress in 1986. She also starred in a TV show later.

Your life will take a new direction the day you decide to take quit blaming everyone for your problems and start taking action towards their solution. Dr. Denis Waitley says, *"I am behind the wheel in my life. Losers let it happen; winners make it happen."* Changing our attitude about problems comes when we realize the all good things come to us through adversity. **"In this life we will encounter hurts and trials that we will not be able to change; we are just going to have to allow them to change us."** Ron Lee Davis.

Candy Lightner made a choice about how to deal with tragedy when her daughter Cari was killed by a drunk driver May 3, 1980. She could have spent the rest of her life mourning, but instead, she made a decision to take action so there would be fewer drunk driving fatalities.

Lightner founded Mothers Against Drunk Driving (Madd), and their first action was to demonstrate in Sacramento California. Next 100 people marched in front of the White House. Today, there are 360 chapters, a national commission against drunk driving, and an impressive 400 new laws in fifty states addressing drunk driving. These new laws are requiring quicker action against first-time drunk drivers and taking away the licenses of habitual drunk drivers. Throught Lightner's initial efforts drunk driving has been reduced by 30%.

"It's the little things that make the big things possible. Only close attention to the fine details of any operation makes the operation first class."

J. Willard Marriot

"What you commit yourself to be will change what you are and make you into a completely different person. Let me repeat that. Not the past but the future conditions you, because what you commit yourself to become determines what you are-more than anything that ever happened to you yesterday or the day before. Therefore I ask you a very simple question: What are your commitments? Where are you going? What are you going to be? You show me somebody who hasn't decided, and I'll show you somebody who has no identity, no personality, no direction." These words on commitment come from Dr. Anthony Campolo, professor of Sociology at Eastern College in Pennsylvania, author, and dynamic speaker.

Problems

John Schnatter founded Papa John's International in Louisville, Kentucky, in 1984 with $1,600 in personal savings. Although he knew his bar would support him adequately, he desired to do bigger things. Papa John's now does $164 million in systemwide sales and $89 million in total revenues.

Part of our problem is that we either think that we are the only person who has problems or that ours are worse than everyone else's. The less you worry about your reputation or failure, the more success you will accomplish. Just as there is abundance in our universe, there is abundance in our world. When business and people think the success or money people acquire limits what they can obtain, they are limiting their world.

Actually, **Mary Tyler Moore** put adversity in perspective when she said, *"Pain nourishes courage. You can't be brave if you've only had wonderful things happen to you."* Strong people look back on the unhappy events that happened in their childhood and see that these occurrences made them strong adults. **Dorothea Dix**, who lived from 1802-1887 was brought up in unhappy and unstable home which she was forced to leave at the age of 10. Later she became involved in helping the mentally ill and worked for the first legislative reforms in their treatment.

If you study the history of most inventions, you will find that they were solutions to problems. Problems then become enormous opportunities. Grenville Kaiser said, *"To every problem there is already a solution, whether you know what it is or not."*

Most successful businesses were started to solve a problem. **Sybil Ferguson's** neighbors saw that she lost 56 pounds and wanted to learn her secrets. A support group began meeting to discuss weight-loss and encourage each other. Seeing the success of this group, Sybil began to franchise the idea, thus The Diet Center with annual revenues of over $45 million developed.

"Anytime there's an occurrence that could be perceived as a negative, we look at it as an opportunity." With an attitude like that, how could Greg Johnston, Pam Walsh and Matt Walsh fail? Our Secret, their company, crafts upscale candles and ironwork candleholders. They began while in college in 1987 with $1,000. They now have sales of $12 million. They <u>know</u> about problems.; Their business burned down twice, but each time they started over again.

Alpine Computer Systems Inc. was started in1988 because **Bob Willis** along with **Michael** and **Tom Sheehan** saw a need for computer-networking services. They started small in 500 square feet of warehouse space and agreed to stuff rubber washers in bottle caps for four hours daily instead of paying rent. They started the business with $300 on a credit card, and today the business does $9 million.

Marilyn Hamilton, owner of Quickie Designs, was injured in a hang gliding accident that left her crippled. She was not able to do all the things she loved in the antiquated wheel chairs, so she called on hang gliding experts to use their technology to improve wheelchairs. The result was lightweight wheel chairs which offered freedom to their owners. Her premise was, "**If you build a dream, the dream builds you.**" Marilyn now spends her time encouraging others who unable to walk to participate in sports and other activities which they once thought were impossible for them. The physically challenged are now encouraged to join clubs and participate in sports activities.

Problems

Eleanor Roosevelt exercised her influence as First Lady as a determined fighter against the war on poverty during the Great Depression. She did not quit her travels to coal mines, hospitals, and speaking engagements once her husband died. She excelled in her appointment to the League of Nations.

Being in a high position makes life no easier. Eleanor Roosevelt suffered shyness and a lack of self-esteem because of her looks, but she continued with dignity despite her doubts coupled with the knowledge that her husband was unfaithful. She was criticized, ostracized, and ignored by those who disagreed with her commitment to human rights.

Marion Anderson was the first black solo singer to appear at the Metropolitan Opera House in New York City. Her voice was described as one that comes in a hundred years. The Daughters of the American Revolution blocked her appearance at Constitution Hall. Instead, Eleanor Roosevelt organized a concert on Easter Sunday for her at Lincoln Memorial, where 75,000 people were able to listen to one of the greatest voices of our time. *"As long as you keep a person down, some part of you has to be down there to hold him down, so it means you cannot soar as you otherwise might. I could not run away from the situation. I had become, whether I liked it or not, a symbol representing my people. I had to appear."*   Marion Anderson

Anderson led the way for other aspiring black opera stars such as **Jessye Norman**, an outstanding soprano for 25 years who rouses near hour-long ovations. She has been awarded honorary doctorates, and an orchid was named after her. She prefers roles where women are strong.

Success Through Spirituality For Women

Find a need and work to change the status quo. **Cardiss Collins,** the longest serving African-American woman in the House of Representatives, works hard requiring the Federal Communications Commission to address the barriers that work against minority and women ownership of communications businesses. The National Foundation for Women Business Owners estimates that there are 6.5 million female business owners.

Lynn Cook is an example of strong survivor. After her divorce she was left with absolutely nothing and forced to go on welfare to support her three children. Later she was able to find better work and was able to get on her feet again, pay off all of her debts, and drop her welfare.

Ann Jones's husband divorced her, and just a few months later she was diagnosed with breast cancer. She was expected to deal with her disease and her pain from the divorce simultaneously. Ann overcame this huge obstacle in her life and went on to get her Master's degree. She also found a new man. Four years later the man she thought had healed her emotionally left her for someone half her age. Then she discovered that would have to have a hysterectomy. She had the operation and has survived. She reports that this has all only made her stronger!

"History has demonstrated that the most notable winners usually encountered heartbreaking obstacles before they triumphed. They finally won because they refused to become discouraged by their defeats. Disappointments acted as a challenge. Don't let difficulties discourage you."

B.C. Forbes

Thank goodness **Susan B. Anthony** was not discouraged by problems or we might not be voting today.

Anthony, who probably is not known as well for her efforts against slavery, made 145 extempore speeches. She wrote four volumes of the **History of Woman Suffrage,** three volumes of the **Life and Work of Susan B. Anthony,** and produced more than one hundred issues of "The Revolution," a radical newspaper. It was difficult to find advertisers because she wrote articles demanding women's suffrage and good treatment. The paper lasted for two years but was finally sold, and Anthony became responsible for a $10,000 debt which was massive in the 1870's. Anthony published her own books in conjunction with Fowler and Wells publishers, but they never made a profit.

Remember **Elizabeth Cady Stanton**, mother of seven, founder of the National Woman's Suffrage Association and Anthony's collaborator, when you use your children as an excuse for not succeeding. She was a woman of strength who offset Anthony's weaknesses. She wrote the "Declaration of the Rights of Women" which changed and charged the movement.

It would take until 1969 before the first Black congresswoman, **Shirley Chisholm**, would be elected to the House of Reprentatives. But she would serve for seven terms, and in 1972 she made a historical bid to become President.

Women should spend time studying the strong women who preceded them instead of watching all the victims complain on talk television. Consider **Anne Marbury Hutchinson** who lived from 1591-1643, had <u>15 children</u> and was still strong enough to hold religious meetings in her home. She was charged and found guilty of sedition, excommunicated from the church, and banished from the colony. Her family moved to New

Netherland where Indians raided her home and killed everyone except one daughter.

We think that women have just started being in combat zones during wars. **Deborah Samson Gannett**, who lived from 1760-1727, enlisted in the Continental Army as a man named Robert Shurtleff. She fought in the American Revolution, and her identity was not discovered until she was hospitalized years later.

Corporations are accused of having **glass and concrete** ceilings. *"The glass ceiling gets more pliable when you turn up the heat."* says Pauline Kezer. It is an artificial barrier put up to keep qualified women from advancing and reaching their potential. **"The Glass Ceiling hinders not only individuals but society as a whole. It effectively cuts our pool of potential corporate leaders by half. It deprives our economy of new leaders, new sources of creativity- the "would be" pioneers of the business world,"** says Lynn Martin.

However, Kraft General Foods has a corporate manager named **Brenda Schofield** who works for affirmative action. She is also general manager of the Corporate Women's Network, a group of 2,000 black female executives and administrators trying to break through the concrete ceiling.

Real estate is a good profession in which women can succeed because it requires a course in selling real estate rather then a college degree. Women who have learned to relate to people, to be creative in their marketing, and who have lots of energy and enthusiasm succeed in real estate.

Robert Rist, President of Coldwell Banker Residential Affiliates Inc. says that women has assumed key leadership roles within the company. Of the 1,229 affiliate companies comprising the Coldwell Banker

Residential Affiliates network of 1,805 offices, 580 franchise broker/owners, 681 franchise company officers or directors, and 471 managers of franchise offices are women. At the corporate level women hold the position of first vice president/director of affiliate services and first vice president/director of franchise development.

Danielle Kennedy, author of *Selling- The Danielle Kennedy Way,* is an energetic, funny motivational speaker who relates stories of her own life in discussing how to be successful in selling real estate. Many of her suggestions would apply to selling anything because she emphasizes using creative marketing techniques, taking time to understand to whom you are trying to sell, and not concerning yourself with trying to compete with other salespeople. Kennedy's story about her fear of public speaking are very funny, but very relative to our own fears. She was once given a toilet because she spent so much time facing one with an upset stomach reacting to fear. She says, *"I could never completely eliminate fear. I still feel fear, but the secret to beating fear is to get comfortable with it. The more you succeed, the more you live with fear. You may think it's the other way around, but you're wrong. Whenever you risk, fear pops up. It like a demon in your mind. The solution is to stare it in the face on carry on. Fear becomes your companion. It may even become an ally, if you learn to live with it. "*

Renee Quiros, a reseller account representative with Symantec, a computer software company, told me at a book signing in Houston that "software is a good field for women because it's only been around about ten years so there isn't a good 'ol boy network yet. "Women can make a great salary because they are dealing with a high volume item that is needed in business. Women are not in the managerial levels yet." I asked her about the seminars the company is doing and she said, "The company is spending really big bucks on sending employees to seminars like the one conducted by the Seven Habits of Highly Effective People group, which lasted four days. But the ideas presented at the seminar have to pervade the whole company for major change to take place." Renee said that one seminar which taught yoga and relaxation was enjoyed the most by the employees.

Tracy Johnson Hendrix opened a furniture business selling bedroom furniture that can not be found anywhere else. Johnson Furniture Co. is bringing in sales of $2 million plus. Her bedroom pieces are available through interior designers and mail order.

> *"You learn that, whatever you are doing in life, obstacles don't matter very much. Pain or other circumstances can be there, but if you want to do a job bad enough, you'll find a way to get it done."* Jack Youngblood

Some people see problems and solutions as only having two alternative choices. Myopic thinking keeps us from seeing the whole picture. Don't spend negative time focusing on problems instead of alternative solutions. The next step is to make assumptions about these alternative choices. We can not only look at them through our own eyes, but through the perspective of buyers, employers, and co-workers.

When we achieve the interdependent thinking in our organizations, relationships and businesses, we are able to work and live with snergy- when creative imaginations are combined and thus produce more solutions or ideas than each person working individually. Stephen Covey says, *"Seek first to understand and then be understood."*

In the same vein, when you present yourself, don't respond to distractions . A spiritually aware person knows that our communications-verbally, body language, mannerisms all reflect the inner thinking of our minds. If we focus on our **purpose**, we will act in a controlled purposeful manner. Everything that we are, our uniqueness, energy, personality and physical attributes tell who we are. We know that most opinions of others are formed in the first four minutes so this is the time to be especially aware of your actions and words.

To have success, professionally and personally, we are always dependent on putting people first-service to others. We are learning the value of individual thinking joined with collaborative thinking is what makes us more competitive in the marketplace and more understanding in our personal lives. Lives that are persistent and committed to the goal of the **full expression** of their purpose will produce great results.

Public television offers great programming that teaches us much about life. One show on how the oil companies became mega corporations and determined our foreign policy in the Mid East was especially informing. During the oil crisis of the 70's Americans had to wait in lines to purchase gas, something they had not had to do since World War II. **President Jimmy Carter** did not light the Christmas tree lights at the White House to stress conservation of energy.

While I do not think we should be wasteful, I think the Carter's actions made the people fear the future. What the oil embargo really did was force the United States and other countries to start seeking other sources of oil such as the North Sea and other countries. A friend of mine from Venezuela had his college tuition paid in the United States because his country's economy improved so much.

As a result, the Mid East countries lost their strong hold on oil prices. New technologies were discovered. We must always have an optimistic view of the future. No problems are so great that we can not use our minds to solve.

While more women are in supervisors positions, they are still locked out of management. Interviewing for a job requires some strategic planning where many women do not know the rules. In many cases, the interviewer is already slanted toward a male candidate, and is looking for a reason to hire him over you. If you were hiring someone for a secretarial position and a male applied, how much opposition to your predisposed thinking would he have to overcome. You may think that there is still no job discrimination if you have been living in the Land of OZ, but you are going to have to fight doubly hard for a good job, and there is no use giving anyone ammunition to use against you.

If you think you are beaten, you are,
If you think that you dare not, you don't,
If you'd like to win, but you think you can't,
It's almost certain you won't.
Anon.

BE A RISK TAKER

"By exposing yourself to risk, you're exposing yourself to heavy-duty learning, which gets you on all levels. It becomes a very emotional experience as well as an intellectual experience. Each time you make a mistake, you're learning from the school of hard knocks, which is the best education available."
                                        Gifford Pinchot

"Woman's discontent increases in exact proportion to her development."
                                        Elizabeth Cady Stanton

"I had a life with options but frequently I lived as if I had none. The sad result of my not having exercised my choices is that my memory of myself is not of the woman I believe I am." How many of us could say the same thing about our lives that Liv Ullman said?

The reason that most people do not become successful is because they have been taught and programmed that it is **wrong** to take risks because they **might** fail. Erica Jong says, **"And the trouble is, if you don't risk anything, you risk even more."** So they continue watching mediocre television, eating mediocre fast food, and having no emotional experiences with success.

> *"The time when you need to do something is when no one else is willing to do it, when people are saying it can't be done."* Mary Frances Berry

Can you imagine being black and riding on a train in 1881 and refusing to move to the "colored section?" **Ida Wills-Barnett**, who lived from 1862-1931, was an active protester against slavery and women's suffrage who stood for her rights as an individual. She was born as a slave in Mississippi but she become educated and taught school. Teenaged girls and grown women these days have the advantage of all the education they want but many do nothing with their opportunities.

Another slave, **Sarah Breedlove Walker** who lived from 1867-1919 was born in Louisiana, orphaned at six, married at 14, and widowed at 20. She worked as a laundress for 20 years, and ,though she was illiterate, she discovered a hair treatment for black women. This enabled her to become the first female African American millionaire.

In 1910 **Alice Stebbins Wells** joined the Los Angeles police department and started her long campaign to get women hired into police work.

Anita Hill had nothing to gain personally by speaking out against Clarence Thomas. The University of Oklahoma law professor decided to testify that her former boss, Thomas, had sexually harassed her. Some of the Senators who were on the all-male Judiciary Committee, now admit that all the facts were not revealed at the hearing. The book, *Strange Justice: The Selling of Clarence Thomas,* presents the other side. Hill's sacrifice and courage revived the women's rights movement and caused the election of large numbers of women to congress in 1992, the "Year of the Woman" in American politics.

"If you think you can, you can. And if you think you can't, you're right. No matter how busy you are, you must take time to make the other person feel important."

Mary Kay Ash

Mary Kay Ash sells skin care products to women who are looking to improve their image and potential for success. **She risked her entire life savings to start her business.** Her first show only produced $1.50 in sales, yet she kept her confidence in the business. She improved her selling techniques, refined the packaging, and adjusted her attitude to succeed. She is now making gross sales over $200 million.

Irma Elder was a housewife until her husband's death in 1983. She needed to send her three children to college so she felt she had no choice but to run the Ford dealership. Under her leadership, Troy Motors went from sales of $35 million in 1983 to currently $364 million. Elder's is one of the largest woman-owned private dealerships. She now realizes she enjoyed being in the business world.

Dian Graves and her husband opened Owen Healthcare in 1969. Seven years later Dian's husband died in an airplane crash. Since Dian took over the business it has grown tremendously, from $6.6 million to $320 million in sales. Owen now provides health-care services in more than 40 states.

Donna and her husband **Norm Reeves** opened one of the first US. Honda dealerships in 1955. Donna took over the business after her husband died in 1973. Norm

Reeves Honda is now the largest dealership with sales about $252 million.

German-born, **Christel DeHaan** believes when you take a risk and choose a new environment, you have to become more resourceful and this is one of the reasons immigrants succeed. She and her former husband started RCI, the world's largest time-share firm. Now as CEO DeHaan runs the company which has 1.7 million members.

Kathy Prasnicki, who is only 33 now, started a business in 1985 called Sun Coast which buys petroleum from independent refineries and supplies it to school districts, corporate fleets, trucking firms, and convenience stores. She could have feared taking the risk because her former employer, Jasper Oil, decided to pull out of that market. Her risk paid off because last year her company did $158 million. She is a single parent of one child.

Risk-taker, **Jane Campion** directed the unconventional film, *"The Piano"*, starring Holly Hunter, Anna Paquin, Harvey Keitel, and Sam Neill. The movie won the Palme d'Or at the Cannes Film Festival. Hunter won best actress and Paquin won best supporting actress.

Vicki Van Meter at age 11 became the youngest person to fly across the United States. Federal regulations required that an instructor accompany Vicki, but she did all the navigating by herself.

"One only gets to the top rung on the ladder by steadily climbing up one at a time, and suddenly all sorts of powers, all sorts of abilities which you thought never belonged to you- suddenly become within your own possibility and you think, 'Well, I'll have a go, too.'" Margaret Thatcher became England's first woman Prime Minister in 1979 and will be its longest serving in the 20th century. Thatcher grew up in an apartment over her father's store where they read books on politics each week.

Susan Butcher was not born in Alaska, but she chose to live there and raise dogs. She set a new course record in winning her fourth Anchorage-Nome Iditarod Trail Sled Dog Race. Because she has conquered a "man's sport," she is a world-wide celebrity. If you get a chance, read about how this lady prepares for this race and the hardships she has to endure. She is amazing.

Another amazing woman was **Marion Rice Hart** who at the age of 61 made her first trans-Atlantic flight in 1953. She made her first solo transatlantic flight in 1966, at age 74.

A movie was made about **Shirley Muldowney**, the first woman to win the National Hot Rod Association Championship of drag racing. She became the first person to win the race two times more. Her first husband divorced her because he wanted her to be a stay-at-home wife. **Janet Guthrie** was the first woman to drive in the Indianapolis 500 automobile race.

Risk taker **Rolonda Watts** worked as an outstanding journalist before she entered the competitive market of television talk shows. Rapidly, her show became syndicated appearing in 70% of the U.S. market and all of the top-10 market stations. Because of her lively personality, her show gained in ratings number 2 to Oprah.

Be Financially Savvy

√ Working women account for $1.04 trillion in annual earnings (34% of all wages and salaries).

√ 2.8 million women earn at least $50,000 a year.

√ We only make 74 cents for every dollar a man earns.

Where have you acquired the knowledge to make your financial decisions? **Most women have pre-conceived ideas about investing and spending that are working against their retaining and obtaining more money.**

Here's some examples of faulty financial thinking.

• Women often purchase an item if they **think** it is discounted. Friends often brag that they saved 40% on a purchase. I ask, 40% of what, or how do they know it was not over-priced in the first place? A chain of stores advertising 50% off expects us to believe that they do not need to pay for rent, employees, and other expenses plus make a profit to stay in business.

- Because you do not lie, you aren't suspicious of liars or those who don't tell the whole truth. Why do you think laws had to be passed that forced real estate agents to reveal that a land dump was being built a mile from the house you were about to purchase? Salespersons use the technique of anchoring, or associating, one item to the value of another.

- Some women are overly cautious when it comes to investing in stocks and mutual funds. But most married women say that they decide with their husbands about which stocks to invest in.

- Women are fearful of investments because they are more concerned about the pain of losing money than the happiness of making money. To invest in mutual funds, go to the library and read the **Morningstar Mutual Funds** information. It provides comprehensive data on 1,240 different funds. It publishes an investment newsletter. (1-800-876-5005) for $65 a year.

- Holding on to something is better than losing it. **No!.** Know when it is better to cut your losses no matter how much time or effort you have invested.

- You can contact the Consumer Credit Counseling Service(1-800-388-2227) for a non-profit credit counseling service near you if you have run up your credit cards too high. They will help you set up a budget and debt repayment plan.
     Any business owner should retain as much ownership of his business as possible for the greatest financial rewards. Oprah Winfrey makes over $53 million a year because she kept control of Harpo and syndicates

her own show. She is the third woman to own a studio. As host of the # 1 talk show on television she fights to maintain integrity with the people and topics on her show. Winfrey is generous with the money she has made. She donates millions to The United Negro College Fund, Morehouse College, and the Harold Washington Library. Oprah Winfrey has proven her diversified interests and larger power by completing a 26-mile marathon. She is also an accomplished actress.

Ann Fudge is the new president of Maxwell House Coffee, which sells about 25% of the U.S. coffee market, and she controls a $1.5 billion in this division of General Foods. Fudge, a Harvard graduate, is described as having marketing savvy.

On the other hand, Sandra Lockhart, former girlfriend of Clint Eastwood for 12 years, found out the hard way what happens when you trust someone else to look after your interests. Lockhart had a promising career as an actress when she met Eastwood. She starred with him in movies for 12 years, but her career became tied in to Eastwoods. One day she found all of her possessions moved out of their home and locks put on the gate. Lockhart said that Eastwood made promises to help her get her career started again by working out a deal with a movie studio and to also compensate her. She dropped the palimony suit and then found that none of the promises took place. She is now suing Eastwood again.

Women, probably more so than men, have picked up negative attitudes toward money. They see the attaining of money as evil, dirty, sinful, and crude. Money is necessary to achieve your purpose in life. Some good books about money are, Slyvia Porter's, **Money Book;** Paula Nelson's, **The Joy of Money, Money Smart; Secrets Women Need to Know About Money** by Esther

Berger; and **How to Turn Your Money Life Around**, by Ruth Hayden.

    The Money Diet, by Ginger Applegarth, offers suggestions for getting your finances in order. As former personal finance correspondent for "The Today Show," she suggests keeping a record of how you spend and then you can begin budgeting. Then you can make some investment decisions.

> *"The more education a woman has, the wider the gap between men's and women's earning for the same work."*   Sandra Day O'Connor

    Because we shy away from math as much as we do dealing with money, women are **short-changing** their acquisition of money. Increase you math skills or at least become more proficient with your calculator. It is necessary for the successful employee and employer to deal with company budgets, income expenses, sales estimates, overhead costs, and that totally necessary world of profit-and-loss. Brilliantly noted, if you aren't willing to deal with the facts and figures of money, don't expect to have any.

    "Women are going to learn how to be providers. I don't mean workers, we're already workers. The difference is taking responsibility not only for your economic present, but for your future. That's a big change. Up to this point, women have been expected to be contributors and helpmates. But relationships and marriage are not predictable any more, so women are starting to pick careers and think about money, lifestyle, location, and how many children to have-everything from A to Z in terms of what they alone can support."   Pepper Schwartz

Be Financially Savy

Margaret Brent, who lived from 1600-1671, was described as a "spinster" and an adept businesswoman by increasing her land holdings. She acted as power of attorney for others because of her renowned speaking abilities. She became the first suffragist when she tried to vote in 1648.

Cathy Hughes had a baby while she was a teenager, but she has gone on to own nine radio stations in Washington, D.C., Baltimore, and Atlanta. She purchased small radio stations with her company, Radio One, Inc. and turned them around. She also has a radio program called **The Cathy Hughes Show.**

Lonear Heard owns seven McDonald's restaurants which grossed $11 million dollars last year. She could have chosen to sell the management corporation her husband owned, but she had prepared herself for the responsibility.

Michele J. Hooper, former president of Baxter Canada, is now president of Caremark's International Business Group, a $1.4 billion division working with expanding the bank's operations in seven countries.

How do you get money to start a business if you don't have any? **Steve and Andi Rosenstein** worked for a surfwear company for years, but did not have money to start their own business. They convinced contractors and suppliers to extend them credit. They now run an upscale casual clothing company of trademark thermal knitwear called Fitiques that sells to specialty boutiques and fine stores. Sales are now at $15 million.

Beth Stewart started a business with no money. Her company sells ad space on the entire surface of street buses. She started the business in 1986 and is now doing $ 2.2 million with customers such as Burger King and ReMax.

Success Through Spirituality For Women

John Egart and David Soderquiest started First Team Sports in Mounds View, Minnesota, in 1985 with $1,000. The company manufactures and distributes in-line roller skates and accessories. The owners did not receive a salary until 1987 when the company went public.

Jules Burt, owner of Jules Jewels, lived in Mexico and when she moved to Atlanta she started selling silver jewelry from Mexico. Then she started showing some of her paintings in her store. Thinking that the painting would like great on tee shirts, she approached a silk screen tee shirt producer and told him she had no money but a great idea. He extended her credit. The tee shirt sales were so successful, she was able to pay him the money owed and order more. I saw the paintings and decided that one would make a great cover for a book.

When you think of the Jenny Craig Company you think of success, but in 1993 the company went from profits of $29.1 million to a $3.4 million deficit. The company closed 30 centers and hired a new CEO. The company's misleading advertisements had to be settled for a $10 million suit charging that their programs were medically unsafe. A sexual discrimination suit of male employees brought further troubles.

SBA Loans and Resources

You have probably eaten a cookie from a Mrs. Fields store. They were started in 1977 by **Debbi Stivyer** with the encouragement of her husband to take out a $50,000 Small Business Administrative loan. There are now more than 600 stores. Debbi was successful because she loved what she was doing, she believed in her product, and she wouldn't take no for an answer. When people did not buy her cookies at first, she gave them out in the streets of Palo Alto, California. Customers flocked to her store then. By the way, friends and family told her it was foolish to go into business.

The Office of Women's Business Ownership has a new pilot loan program. This program allows the SBA to guarantee a loan before the entrepreneur even approaches a bank. The pilot will last one year, and become permanent if successful.

For businesses needing loans for $25,000 or less, the SBA offers the Microloan Program. Nearly 60% of these loans go to women and minorities. A microloan is an excellent starting point because it allows you to build up a track record.

Women own 38% of the 20 million U.S. small businesses. On the other hand, women now only receive 8% to 10% of the Small Business Administration's guaranteed loans. Most women starting their own businesses do not know about the SBA or how to fill out the forms. The SBA is making it easier for women to get loans. Last year the SBA loaned $ 6.4 billion.

The first step is to go through a nonprofit intermediary agency, or business development center, in your area. For many women, this is their first venture in entrepreneurship, which means the business does not have a financial history. The loan is based on the woman's ability to make the business successful.

The good news is the SBA offers a Microloan Program for businesses needing less than $25,000. About 60% of these loans go to women and minorities. Using your computer, you can dial the SBA bulletin board. It contains material explaining business plans and writing each section and information on loans.

Lillian Lincoln, the first black woman to earn an MBA from Harvard and the first woman elected president of the Building Services Contractors Association International, is founder and President of Centennial Once Inc. With the help of an SBA program to secure a $12,000 line of credit and $4,000 of her own money, she secured a contract with the federal government. Her company now does sales of $10.5 million.

This is a great time to try for an SBA loan because the approval record is running 20% above last year's record. The **Loc Doc program** cuts paperwork down to one page and has a two-day turnaround on requests for SBA guarantees on loans of less than $100,000. A commercial lender makes the actual loan, but the SBA can guarantee up to 90 percent of it which makes a big difference when it comes to approval. The GreenLine program is a reliable short-term source of working capital. The SBA guarantees up to 75% of revolving lines of credit, extended by commercial lenders for as much as five years and $750,000. GreenLine has helped many small businesses cover revolving credit needs for companies doing manufacturing and contracting. GreenLine allows continuous borrowing and repayment during the five-year loan period.

The SBA has founded a new program called **Women's Network for Entrepreneurial Training,**

SBA Loans and Resources

(WNET) which is designed to foster year-long mentoring relationships between fledgling women-owned businesses and successful women-owned businesses of 1 to 3 years .

Pennsylvania is a good example of a state promoting entrepreneurs. In one 45,000-square-mile area, 100 percent of the new jobs were in small businesses. Of the 277,000 enterprises in the state, 277,000 were small businesses. The SBA there offers workshops called **"Starting and Managing a Small Business of Your Own."** It also provides publications and videotapes on marketing, winning customers and personnel management.

Free Support Services

The following free support services are aids to small businesses.

1. The Service Corps of Retired Executives (SCORE) This is a free counseling service for start up or ongoing businesses. Staffed by retired executives, they can provide you with assistance in business, planning, marketing, and sales.

2. The Small Business Answer Desk (1-800-368-5855). The Small Business Administration (SBA) 's toll free number to obtain general information and referrals to SCORE services, other SBA services. *The Directory of Federal & State Business Assistance* costs $29 $3 plus handling . It lists more than 180 federal and 500 assistance programs. This directory tells you how to find free management consulting, how to obtain mailing list prospects, provide information on finding funding, and more. SBA offers services and resources such as: Business loans, assisting small high-technology firms, special small businesses, and other programs. SBA has various books and pamphlets to help people which are very inexpensive or free.

3. Office of Women's Business Ownership (WBO). Each state has an an office which gives information about federally funded programs for small business. Loan information meetings are held to describe the loan programs available through the SBA. The mentor program matches experienced businesswomen with new business women.

4. Small Business Institutes (SBI). Existing small businesses are provided management assistance. Your business becomes a class or individual project for college seniors or graduate students.

5. Small Business Development Centers (BDCs). The SBDC helps you get advice from community resources, like attorneys, accountants, and other consultants.

Look up the Small Business Administration in your phone book to contact these organizations.

124

SBA Loans and Resources

(**SCORE**) Service Corps of Retired Executives helped **Richard** and **Sharon Rose** with marketing, finance, and management The first year they started Sharon's Finest in 1987. The Santa Rosa, California, company develops and markets health foods such as tofu-based cheeses. They made nothing for the first year, but now revenues are $3 million.

The **Women's Self-Employment Project (WSEP)** focuses on microenterprise development, businesses that require less the $5,000 to start. The program started in Chicago with low income women, where approximately 85% were African American, 4% Latina, and 11% Caucasian. Since 1986 WSEP has provided business training, technical assistance, and over $500,000 in loans. They have started businesses in accounting, clothing design clothing, catering, and selling. It became a model for economic development programs nationwide. The Sara Lee Foundation honored WSEP with the Chicago Spirit award Winner and $50,000. WSEP offers borrowers 12 weeks of business training, monthly seminars, and two loan programs, which have default rates of 0 to 5%. Women in poverty often live isolated lives and being in business has created a new network of independent women.

Common Cause Magazine featured an article about **Debra Davis** who received at $1,200 loan and was able to buy an industrial sewing machine, fabric and notions to jump-start her clothing design business. She approached Spielgel catalog about selling her 3-D caps. They ordered. She now employs three part-time employees.

For more information, contact the **Women's Self-Employment Projects** at 166 W. Washington, Ste 730, Chicago, IL, 60602 or phone (312-606-8355).

ORGANIZATIONS FOR WOMEN IN BUSINESS AND THE PROFESSIONS

NATIONAL GROUPS OF GENERAL INTEREST

American Business Women's Association
9100 Ward Pkwy
PO Box 8728
Kansas City, MS 64114
(816) 361-6621

American Woman's Economic Development Corporation
641 Lexington Ave
NY, NY 10022
(212) 688-1900

American Women in Enterprise
71 Vanderbilt Ave, 3rd floor
NY, NY 10169
(212) 692-9100

The Committee of 200
625 N. Michigan Ave, Suite 500
Chicago, IL 60611
(312) 751-3477

Executive Women International
515 S 700 East, Suite 2E
Salt Lake City, UT 84102
(801) 355-2800

Federation of Organizations for Professional Women
2001 S Street, NW Suite500
Washington, DC 20009
(202) 328-1415

SBA Loans and Resources

The International Alliance
8600 La Salle Rd, Suite 617
Baltimore, MD 21286
(410) 472-4221

International Network for Women in Enterprise and Trade
PO Box 6178
McLean, VA 22106
(703) 893-8541

Management Training Specialist
550 Bailey, Suite 210
Fort Worth, TX 76107
(817) 332-3612

National Association for Female Executives
127 W. 24th St, 4th Floor
NY, NY 10011
(212) 645-0770

National Chamber of Commerce for Women
10 Waterside Plaza, Suite 6H
NY, NY 10010
(212) 685-3454

The National Federation of Business and Professional Women's Clubs
2012 Massachusetts Ave, NW
Washington, DC 20036
(202) 293-1100

National Women's Economic Alliance
1440 New York Ave NW
Suite 300
Washington, DC 20005
(202) 393-5257

Women in Management
30 North Michigan Ave, Suite 508
Chicago, IL 60602
(312) 263-3636

National Association of Negro Business and Professional Women
1806 New Hampshire Avenue, N.W.
Washington D.C. 20009
(202) 483-4206

National Association of Women Business Owners
1377 K. Street, N.W., Suite 637
Washington, DC 20005
(301) 608-2590

The National Foundation for Women Business Owners
1377 K. Street, N.W., Suite 637
Washington, DC 20005
(301) 495-4975 or (301) 495-4979
(Research and education)

National Women's Business Council
409 Third Street S.W., Suite 7425
Washington D.C. 20024
(202) 205-3850

National Federation of Business and Professional Women's Clubs (202-293-1100)

Women's World Banking (212-768-8513)

The National Association of Black Women Entrepreneurs is headed by **Marilyn Hubbard** who helps the 3,000 members with networking and a support system.

SBA Loans and Resources

Association of Black Woman Entrepreneurs is headed by **Dolores Ratcliffe**. (213) 624-8639

American Business Women's Association
9100 Ward Parkway
PO Box 8728
Kansas City, MO 64114
(816) 361- 6621
Carolyn B. Elman, Executive Director
     This organization provides opportunities for businesswomen to help themselves and others grow personally and professionally through leadership, education, networking support, and national recognition. It offers leadership training and discounted Career Track programs, a resume service, credit card and member loan programs, and various travel and insurance benefits. Publishes CONNECT, a bimonthly newsletter.

     Call the **State Office of Economic Development** to find out if your state has special programs for small businesses. The **State Women's Business Advocates** are very helpful. The group stays current on organizations, educational opportunities, programs, legislation, and government procurement opportunities.

Small Business Sourcebook (Gale Research Company)
Call directly to 800-223-GALE. The book is expensive, but it can be found in large libraries or university business school libraries. It is an excellent book to use on starting a new business.

Wisconsin Innovation Service Center
Contact the Program Manager 414-472-1365

This service center provides you with a evaluation for your invention at a low price. This evaluation is comprehensive and confidential.

Mailing List Brokers Look in the Yellow Pages under "Mailing Lists" to find a person or organization who might be interested in buying your product or using your service. This way you can target your market. Each list is directed to a specific market, such as women over 40 who earn more than $50,000 a year.

Patent and Trademark Office-703-557-3158 (General Information)
Find out whether your idea for a new product has already been registered for a patent, or find out the use of the trademarks. Contact the US Patent Office.

Working Woman Magazine co-sponsors the Annual Professional & Business Women's Conference. For information call 415-548-2424.

The National Association of Insurance Women's Annual Convention is in June. Call 800-766-6249

A new statewide program in Ohio helps women business owners to have greater access to procurement opportunities. *Market Your Assets* requires all state agencies to encourage female entrepreneurs to bid on contracts. It provides equal access to management, technical, financial and procurement assistance; offers business-related education, training, counseling and information; and identifies and develops qualified women-owned companies. To enroll in the program, call *Market Your Assets* at (614) 466-4965.

Your local library has a **Book of Associations** which lists the names and addresses of various groups you might want to join.

Sources For Information

Many women have moved from a succession of parental caretakers to husband caretakers and have never learned how to do a business entirely on their own. You must first set your attitude to believe that if others can do it, "I can do it," and that like everything else, it is just a matter of learning how to follow the correct steps to achieving your goals. I meet people who say that they don't know what they want to do which is hard to imagine since there are around 37,000 ways to make a living! We need to feel a responsibility in the areas of creating schools which teach **thinking**, ecological concerns such as non-polluting energy resources, support for independent and small businesses, cures for diseases, improved health care, and help with emotional and mental problems. **We must be willing to take personal initiative for our concerns and quit expecting others to do our thinking and our jobs.**

You will find state and federal organizations listed in the next section to help you. They are there to provide counsel and advice. They are not going to write your business plan, make your projections, or do a market study. Your husband or friends can't do this for you either. You have to be the one to talk to your banker or other sources of money.

The best way to get help is to ask for it. People don't expect anyone to know about areas where they have not worked. Major corporations make major mistakes with all their expert advice. Coca Cola's attempt to get the American public to switch over to New Coke after they had been drinking Classic Coke most of their lives was not a stroke of brilliance. General Motors' lack of development in the small cars cost them millions.

Be honest with counselors about what you do and don't understand. Make a list of the specific questions and topics you need to discuss. Do your homework before you talk to counselors so that you will make the most of your time.

Call the *State Office of Economic Development* to find out if your state has special programs for small businesses. The State Women's Business Advocates are very helpful. The office stays current on organizations, educational opportunities, programs, legislation, and government procurement opportunities.

Infotrac is one of the most popular systems used to find library information. Infotrac indexes over 1,100 popular journals. Infotrac searches 10 years of back issues to identify articles covering the subjects you enter. This source offers an index to articles published in the *New York Times*. The user looks up key words such as a subject or a person's name, and the index provides a brief summary of all pertinent articles published giving the date of publication and page. Twice every month supplements are issued. You can find this index in practically every library.

Readers' Guide to Periodical Literature
This guide indexes articles published in about 200 popular magazines such as *Newsweek, Health, Ms.,*

Sports Illustrated, and *Popular Science.* This guide is found in most libraries; supplements are issued monthly. The user looks up key words or subjects he or she is interested in.

The Magazine Index (Information Access Company)
This system is an index to about 400 general-interest magazines. The user is provided a display of the index on a special automated terminal. This system is comprehensive and easy to use. The terminal is already loaded with the microfilmed index. You can advance or rewind the index until you come to the subject you are interested in. For any articles listed full bibliographic data is provided.

Business Periodicals Index
This is an index to articles published in nearly 300 periodicals oriented toward business. This index ranges from advertising and marketing to real estate, computers, communications, finance, and insurance. Supplements are issued monthly. This index is found in most libraries. It indexes periodicals that contain information topics beyond the scope of what most people consider simply business; for example, *Journal of Consumer Affairs, Human Resource Management, Telecommunications,* and *Automotive News.* Periodicals like these provide more specialized and in-depth information than the popular magazines indexed in the *Readers' Guide,* but the articles are not overly technical or hard to read. *Business Periodicals Index* is a balance for the information seeker who is not an expert in the field but still wants more than a superficial examination of a subject.

Subject Guide to Books in Print

This is a standard guide for finding books in print on any subject. (Books "in print" are kept in stock by the publisher and can be ordered at a bookstore.) SGBIP lists old and new books: hardbound, paperback, trade, test, adult, and juvenile that are currently in print, by subject. Most libraries and bookstores carry this guide.

Forthcoming Books lists those books that have just been released or are projected to be released within five months. You can find this guide in most bookstores and in large libraries. Supplements are issued bimonthly. *Forthcoming Books* identifies what books are about to be published in a given field. This is especially useful when you are digging up information on a timely issue and you want to find the very latest books.

Sources for Business and Industry Information

Wall Street Journal Index

This is a two-part index arranged by company or subject . All articles published in *The Wall Street Journal* and *Barron's* can be accessed through this index.

Predicasts Funk & Scott Index (Predicasts Inc.)

This is a guide to published articles about industries and about companies' activities and developments. Articles published in leading business periodicals can be indexed through this and the weekly and monthly supplements that are available.

SBA Loans and Resources

Standard & Poor's Register of Corporations, Directors and Executives

A directory of company information presented in three volumes. Volume one is a straight alphabetical listing of approximately 50,000 corporations.

Planning A Business

A study by the National Foundation for Women Business owners says that women-owned businesses are one of the fastest growing segments of the US. economy. The Small Business Administration (SBA) counts about 5 million women-owned businesses, and predicts women will own nearly 40 percent (others say half) of small businesses by 2000.

In 1990 women-owned businesses employed 11 million people and the *Fortune* **500,** 12.3 million. But the *Fortune* **500** is losing at least 200,000 to 300,000 jobs every year. (Since 1980 the 500 big companies have lost 400,000 a year). Although there are no exact numbers, it is a well-established trend that women-owned businesses are creating new jobs every year, as new businesses are formed and as established ones expand. Even if women-owned businesses had hired no one since 1990-a complete impossibility- 1992 would still be the cross-over year when women-owned businesses employed more people than the *Fortune* **500.**

Entrepreneurial Woman says California, Arizona, Colorado, Florida, Illinois, Massachusetts, Minnesota, New York, Pennsylvania, and Wisconsin are the best ten states for women owned businesses.

The track record of women in business is great.
* In 1977, 2 million female-owned businesses had $25 billion in sales. By 1988 women owned 5 million businesses with revenues of $83 billion.
* From 1980 to 1988 the number of entrepreneurs increased 56% overall, but female entrepreneurs grew 82 %.
*In the same time frame entrepreneurial revenues grew

56 % overall, but those of female entrepreneurs soared 129 %.

1) Define the business idea

Write a description of the business idea. This is the most important and difficult part of the business plan because we see that ideas are easy, but knowing how to carry them out requires knowledge in that area. Spending time clarifying the business objectives of the project will help avoid confusion later on. Women at times start businesses because they will be fun, which is fine, but to be purposeful, they must also be profitable. In order to write this description, the business must be completely and clearly thought out. Do your homework!

2) Establish goals and objectives

Commit to writing the series of goals or objectives that should be satisfied by the business venture. If you are going into business with others or have investors, you need to make sure everyone's goals and objectives are in alignment. Keep your customer in mind because that's who you are giving your service.

3) Evalute ideas, objectives, and goals

Analyze carefully whether your basic objective and ideas make sense, whether or not they can work, and whether or not they can fulfill the series of goals and objectives identified in the preceding step. Some people jump on the first idea and don't think out if this is something they want to do all the time or if it will be fulfilling. You definitely don't want to get tied down to a business that is won't let you demonstrate your talents and knowledge. Is this business going to bring you contentment and happiness?

4) Find cash needs

This book has cited various businesses that have been started on a few hundred dollars which is possible. On the other hand, lots of businesses get started and then the owners find out they have cash flow problems when they try to expand. Figure out how to get as much money as you need to start your business. Be realistic about equipment, other initial cash needs, and the amount of working capital necessary. Other people are not going to be excited to work in your business for little pay. If you find investors, more than likely, you will need to ask them for more funding as the business progresses and shows stability. If your kind of business is already established, it would be a good idea to work in a successful business and a not so successful business so that you can see what makes the difference.

I drove behind a just purchased used flashy Cadillac the other day that gave me a laugh.. The car tag had not arrived yet, so it had the car lot's advertisement, "The Credit King, We Will Finance Anyone." We, too, go around wearing the attitude that we are busted but trying to put on fake appearances. Know internally that you have worth, and that you have power that your mind can access.

5) Know for sure where you are going to get the money

This is not time for pie in the sky thinking. Like most women, you probably will have to draw on your creative thinking and ask help from the universe.

6) Write a business plan

Writing a business plan is not jotting ideas on a napkin. Spend a long time meditating about your new business. Daydream during the day and dream at night about solutions and problems. Use all your psychic abilities to pick out a location, do creative funding, buy the right equipment, locate the best materials, and find the best employees.

As the original ideas become more specific, you will face additional problems, which you can welcome because they will cause you to uncover more of your strengths. If you look at problems as opportunities to grow, you do not waste time being frustrated because you know ways to find out answers. You have models, mentors, sources of information, and divine guidance to guide your thinking.

So you've come up with a great idea for a new business. Now where do you go and how do you get started. If you are tempted to skip this section on writing a business plan, **don't**! Federal Express, whose venture capital is over $ 70 million, does a business plan every year. If you are not willing to research and plan your business, you shouldn't waste your time starting it.

Planning A Business

The benefits of writing your plan are:

1.) You decide how you are going to conduct your business, how are you going to market, finance and operate your business.

2.) You have a reference to review how your business is progressing. A business owner has so many areas to spend her time, sometimes the business gets off course. If you are conscious of your time, your plan will tell you how to get back on course.

3.) Most importantly, this is where and how you decide you are going to raise operating money (venture capital).

4.) If you have a business partner, this is a good place to define your agreement.

You need to read a book on writing a business plan, but here are some quick tips. Be optimistic and realistic. Be businesslike, organized and to the point. Here's a good place to use your graphics expertise. It is as important for small companies to write a plan as large ones because they have less operating capital.

A good business plan should include: an **executive summary, company description, market analysis descriptions, strategy and implementation, financial plan and a management and organization description.** Three new business plan software packages are available: Business Plan Pro (for Windows), Palo Alto Software Inc., 1-800-229-7526, PFS Business Plan SoftKey International Inc, 1-800-227-5609, Planmaker Power Solutions For Business, 1-800-955-3337. *The Successful Business Plan: Secrets and Strategies,* by Rhonda

Abrams, has work sheets and good quotes. The book is thorough and organized.

If you decide to **incorporate your business** you can do your own with Unabridged Software's *Incorporate*. A map of the U.S. is shown in the software for users to click on their state. The software creates documents and area-specific information about fees and contact numbers. It goes through a series of questions and drafts an article of incorporation. The price is $69 and you can call 1-800-248-7630.

Suggested readings:

When Friday Isn't Payday: *A Complete Guide to Starting, Running-and Surviving in-a Very Small Business,* by Randy Kirk, a small-business owner, who offers practical options about business problems from his own experiences.

*The Starting and Operating a Business in...*series, Michael D. Jenkins and the Entrepreneurial Services Group of Ernst & Young. This is not an exciting book because it describes the common federal regulatory requirements small business people need to know. Each state has a separate edition on the laws and regulations for that location. But it has the kind of information you NEED.

How to Prepare for Your Business

1. **Learn**

Before you open or start any kind of business, spend as much time as you can finding out everything you can. You will be pleasantly surprised that the knowledge you absorb will come to you when you need it. Gallop Polls show that high income people read an average of 19 books a year. It has been said that the person who can read and doesn't has no advantage over the person who can't read.

Jim Rohn is a motivational speaker who advocates that to be a high achiever we must read and discipline ourselves to read two books a week, or about 100 a year. **"If you've done that for the last 10 years, you're 1,000 books ahead. If you haven't you're 1,000 books behind."**

The following two books would be good reading. *Working Solo: The Real Guide to Freedom and Financial Success with Your Own Business,* Terri Lanier. This book really relates to my situation because it talks about individuals who work alone in the computer age, all the possibilities and problems. Lanier talks about on-line networks, marketing, and time management. Fred Steingold, author of, *The Legal Guide for Starting and Running a Small Business,* covers problems such as negotiating a lease to picking out a location in a clear and sensible manner.

Learn to develop good communication skills, both talking and listening. The more you listen, the more knowledge you add, giving your intuitive mind more to build on. If you don't have a strong self-image, you will lack the confidence in your abilities and won't listen to your inner voice.

Martha Stewart, author of ten books still in print which have sold millions, has her own magazine and television show called *Martha Stewart Living.* She says that she has always relied on her own instincts to become successful. But she decided to enlist **Charlotte Beers,**

chair and chief executive of Ogilvy & Mather, entertainment lawyer Allen Grubman, and Sharon Patrick, a former Mc Kinsey & Company partner, to negotiate a contract between Stewart and Time Inc. Smart women know how to surround themselves with experts. Stewart's new enterprises include entering interactive-media called "Interactive Martha", a Martha Stewart catalog, or maybe a chain of stores. She has a written mission statement that focuses on the areas of her interests.

Frances Hesselbein, was until 1990 the National Executive Director of the Girl Scouts, the largest nonprofit organization for girls and women in the world,. She went from running a troop of 30 girls, to becoming president of her local council, to training board members. **At that point she began reading everything she could about management.** In 1976 she became the head of the Girl Scouts which has 750,000 volunteers, 500 paid staff, and an annual budget of $26 million dollars.

She reorganized the Girl Scouts using the marketing techniques and internal surveys she had read about. Two new programs, Safe Time, which keeps latchkey children busy after school and Daisy Girl Scouts, for five-year-olds in conjunction with Head Start were formed. Her management practices have been modeled by several other organizations. She now lectures, writes, and serves on various boards. Management experts say that Frances Hesselbein could run any major company in the United States.

More good advice is to **learn one new technique a day.** Then, put it into practice at least twice as soon as you learn it. I try to learn something new about my computer almost every day because it is the mainstay of my business. We all enjoy reading, but since we have so much to learn about our businesses, I would suggest that we spend our reading time in the business section or trade magazines.

In my business, I spend a great deal of time keeping up with new books being published, new store openings, reviews, author interviews, marketing tactics, and the latest computer software and technology dealing with books. I read *Publishers Weekly, The New York Times Book Review of Books, Small Press, Working Woman,* and several other magazines when they have pertinent articles on women. I alternate reading about four books at once because I find that I can read for longer periods of time if I switch subjects. To be successful, you must keep up with the new thinking and technology in your field.

As we've learned, old ideas will not succeed in a new market. Leon Martel, in *Mastering Change, the Key to Business Success,* describes how past thinking keeps us from using change:

1. Believing that yesterday's solutions will solve today's problems.
2. Assuming present trends will continue.
3. Neglecting the opportunities offered by future change.

Job Shift, by William Bridges, discusses the changes at American corporations that have eliminated thousands of positions. These workers could learn a new trade and adapt, possibly by becoming consultants or opening their own business.

Competing for the Future, is written by two business professors, Gary Hamel and C.K. Prahalad. This book is about the changes that take place in American corporations. The book focuses on what companies should do to compete on a global level. The two authors review industries that will dominate other companies in the coming years.

144

CompuServe's Entrepreneurial/Small Business has information on topics such as getting a new business located under the Working from Home forum. You can also find business plans that can be down-loaded free of charge.

2. Listen

I frequently drive to book signings in other states because it gives me the opportunity to listen to motivational and inspirational tapes without distractions. After each trip, I'm on such a high because of the new information I have picked up from the tapes, and people in the book business and women I meet at the book signings.

All businesses have so much in common you can learn from everyone you talk to, if you are willing to ask questions and listen. When we start a new business, we are so excited that we want to tell others about it. But how much do you learn from hearing yourself? Being aware of everything going on around you makes you conscious of how you can apply what you are learning to improving and opening up your life. David McNally in *Even Eagles Need a Push*, says, **"Life is meant to be a never-ending education, and when this is fully appreciated, we are no longer survivors but adventurers."**

3. Organize

We are responsible for how we spend our time, money and energy. Consciousness makes you constantly aware of making the best decisions in these areas. Free thinking gives you the chance to work most efficiently because you are most inspired at that time, but you must prepare your materials ahead so that you don't miss a moment of creative thinking. A creative thinker knows that she doesn't need just ideas, but she must be realistic about turning the ideas into profitable situations.

An entrepreneur needs to constantly be aware of her environment for new opportunities. What changes are taking place in the lifestyles, demographics, buying philosophy, government regulations, and competition close at hand and nationally? Listen to the public's and your own complaints and needs in finding new business ventures. She needs to be open to the unexpected events, successful or unsuccessful, that happen in her business and look at them as opportunities.

4. Expand your thinking

I see businesses that name themselves after their street location or their city. Obviously they never plan to move, franchise, or have a second location. Mrs. Winners had to change its name from Granny's Fried Chicken when the company began to expand into other markets. As a natural course, businesses take on selling or servicing in other areas. This is when you don't want to be too set in your thinking because you will miss golden opportunities. If you check out the history of most businesses, they have been in constant flux because of new trends, attitudes, inventions, and needs. If your belief system sees you as small time, you will stay small time. Never be apologetic about where you are starting because everyone had a beginning point.

5. Desire success

None of us would ever tell anyone that we were intentionally trying to fail, but if we do not believe in our own self worth and the worthiness of our purpose, we will sabotage our own success as sort of a fulfillment of prophecy. If you play the old tapes of your detractors that say you will never succeed, then you won't. We are to be *"new creatures"* which means we have the ability each day to act and be what we want to be. Just as our physical bodies are in constant cell replacement, our minds and thinking are in constant change and growth. We can never stay the same because we are constantly receiving new information, but we can be in charge of how we judge the new information. Our minds are not just sponges of words, ideas, and insights. They are originators of thoughts, truths, and beliefs. **So much information is inundating our lives that we must focus on informing ourselves with knowledge that benefits our lives.**

6. Take educated action

I have a lot of women say to me that they would like to do something special with their lives, but they haven't taken the first step toward any action. They sit in dreamland waiting for someone to take their hand. **Doing anything in life begins by beginning.** Two things to remember: If one person has learned something, anyone else can. And I think this applies to being successful. If other people are successful in an area, you can be successful too. Read the section on how your brain works.

Planning A Business

Many women fail to assert themselves when it comes to speaking up for themselves. We defeat ourselves because we fear to ask or demand, to say no, to confront others, or to assert authority.

When you are seeking a new job, an SBA loan, or presenting a marketing plan, you must be able to talk about your abilities and accomplishments in as much detail as possible and with an air of confidence. We have been playing the role of the "good little girl" so long, we think that promoting oneself is bragging. Be honest with others about what you can do and what you want to do in life.

We are all marketing ourselves no matter what kind of business we're in and most of the same principles apply. Businesses strive for a consistent look in their stationery, logo, advertising. You should also present a consistent image that reflects you and your purpose.

Larry Dean was able to get into Georgia Tech with a 750 SAT score a few years ago. That score would not get you into any kind of major school these days. But Larry Dean graduated from college, worked in the banking business, and started a company called SSI which combined banking, computers, and automatic bank teller machines. He used his brain to think of an idea how to help people in the banking business. His company is spiritually-oriented which is reflected in his attitude toward his employees, business environment, and business practices. By the way, Larry Dean lives in a $40 million dollar estate in Atlanta that is a reflection of his spirituality.

Many entrepreneurs are seeing their businesses as having a good influence on society. Businesses now have more resources, more creativity, and energy to change people's lives and help society. Joel Makowe, author of

Beyond the Bottom Line: Putting Social Responsiblity to Work for Your Business and the World, sees **"a gradual shift of power from government to business is a dominant force in our society."**

If you don't have a healthy society and few social problems, businesses will not succeed. There is a direct link to them and a business's bottom line. Business owners who were socially responsible responded to their life experiences and value systems. Now businesses are seeing social responsibility and service to humanity as a market-driven issue.

Alan Reder, author of *In Pursuit of Principle and Profit: Business Success Through Social Responsibility,* writes that there are more good citizens in the business world and more information available to consumers about who is and who is not a good business citizen for people to turn to. He cites examples where people cared enough to make a difference, like keeping dolphins from being caught in tuna nets.

The National Foundation for Women Business Owners (NFWBO) and **Dun & Bradstreet Information Services** report that 7.7 million women-owned businesses generate nearly $1.4 trillion in sales and employ 15.5 million people in the United States. These statistics show that women entrepreneurs are stable and creditworthy. Backing this up is a survival rate of a whopping 72% compared with 66.6 % for US. businesses overall. Women business owners are disproving the idea that their companies are credit risky. Almost 60% of women-owned businesses were ranked a low credit risk.

The good news is that women who start businesses have a good chance to succeed. Women are more cautious than men in business because they aren't trying to conquer the world with their first venture. They are more "strategic" risk-takers, and because of their financial circumstances, have to be more resourceful and have greater resolve, especially as circumstances become more difficult.

This fact is backed up by a study by the Avon Corporation and New Work Decision, a research firm. **Janet Harris-Lange**, President of the National Association of Women Business Owners, says that **women business owners are *more likely to succeed*** because women admit they need help and surround themselves with good people. Women strongly interrelate with and reinforce one another. A woman who has a strong and complex sense of her own identity willingly shares information. She is able to see a picture of the world rather than just her business or organization because she has participated in activities which had nothing to do with jobs.

Note the words women use: interaction, flow, access, feel, conduit, reach, touch, involvement, network. These are relational and process words that focus on doing tasks rather than on completion of tasks. Today's companies are structured less formally. Instead of the 80's hierarchical structure, innovative companies are seeking to allocate decision-making to the managers. Today's focus is on innovation and fast-paced information exchange.

"I couldn't find a conduit through my work to do some of the things I thought were socially relevant. The companies I worked for didn't have the same values. I decided to leave corporate work and start a company of my own, where I could integrate personal and social values into a business ethic," said Debbie Aguirre who started Tierra Pacifica Corp. in 1992. The company contributes a project to each city in which it does business. It has built a battered women's shelter, housing projects, and a library reading corner for seniors.

A spiritual woman does not feel the need to compete with others; she is focusing on doing the best job she can. She will feel a greater comfort around people who have a sense of fulfilling a higher purpose rather than material conquests. Value is placed on vision and the ability to think creatively. The spiritual woman is open-minded and flexible. She is willing to look at both sides of an issue and see through the other person's eyes. With this understanding of people, she knows to motivate others to fulfill the intended purpose. This woman has a thirst for knowledge and is always looking for new ideas. Since the focus is service to others, she is always looking for new and better ways. Some businesses are seeking to be more ecological, while stressing the interrelation of all things.

"A woman would no more let her business fail than she would let someone kill her child," says Beatrice Fitzpatrick, founder and president of the American Women's Economic Development Corporation in New York , which has assisted or trained 100,000 women in the past 15 years. Women who seek service as their goal know that basic human needs do not change. Motherhood makes women good managers because they have learned the skills of: organization, balancing, teaching, leading, guiding, handling disturbances and conflicts, giving detailed instructions, and patience. Women more often work at tasks that are cyclical and unending. Thus they are more process-oriented which causes them to concentrate on the process rather than the final achievement.

Because women are often responsible for running their homes and working full-time, they have to balance their work and family lives. Unlike men, they do not compartmentalize their lives which many women feel gives them greater energy because their lives are not limited and they are not cut off from outside interests. Men who have been extremely successful in businesses often show feelings of depression, emptiness, and dissatisfaction in their lives. They fulfilled their desire for power and forgot their goals and dreams. They work hard but their lives have lost their sense of **awareness**.

CNN did a show about a " College for Candidates" held at Harvard University to help women learn how to run for elected office. Surveys of both males and females showed that many voters chose women candidates because they believed that they had more integrity and less ego.

In preparation for a bid for mayor, **La Verne Mitchell** attended the course in campaign basics: how to raise funds, dress, attract media coverage and counter smear tactics. Lincoln Heights, home for La Verne, is the first all-black incorporated city in the United States. She won a city council post, but lost the next election when she supported a pre-release center for convicts in hopes that the city would gain access to minority contracting jobs to raise money for the city.

Lois Working has worked for Ford Motors in Fairfield, Ohio, for 15 years and is a member of the United Auto Workers. She ran for local union representative and became the first woman elected because she thought changes should be made. She rebuked criticism for not being tough enough by surviving the tragedy of having her only son killed by a drunk driver just before the election and not turning to alcohol or drugs.

Check out the On-Line Resources such as **American On-line's Microsoft Small Business Center.** It has articles from magazines, organizations' literature, videotape transcripts on topics such as Finance, Starting a business, and Women in business. I checked out **"Alternative Ways to Find Capital"** and **"Alternative Financing"** to print this book.

Financing Sources for Women- Owned Businesses

Women's Equity Fund (303) 443-2620

Capital Rose (215) 667-1666

Inroads Capital Partners (312) 902-6347

National Association of Female Executive/Venture Capital Fund (212) 477-2200

Sky Venture Fund (615) 248-1249

Some selected reading about opening a business

Dive Right In- The sharks Won't Bite, Jane Wesman offers advice to women starting a business. The book offers basic information about hiring the right people and negotiating.

Women-Owned Businesses: The New Economic Force, 1992 Data Report, National Foundation for Women business Owners (Washington, D.C., 1993)

Our Wildest Dreams: Women Making Money, Doing Good, Having Fun, Joline Godfey

Taking Control of Your Life: The Secrets of Successful Enterprising Women, Gail Blanke and Kathleen Walas

Formulate A Marketing Plan

For 10 years I owned a gift shop, which means that I did everything from purchasing, shelving, and marketing, to sweeping the store. Being a novice store owner, I made a lot of marketing mistakes that I hope you will avoid.

First, I tried to be too many things for too many people. You must decide which market you are going after and focus on it. Second, I tried to have everything that the other stores had instead of selling merchandise no one else had. As with people, stores have to find their uniqueness. Thirdly, I spend time doing things that had a sense of urgency but were not necessarily the most important things. Taking the time to plan marketing strategies several weeks in advance takes discipline and is not immediate gratification, but it pays the big dividends. The same holidays, the time that you really make your money, are around the same time each year so you have time for creativity and planning.

As an author/publisher, I have the total responsibility of marketing my books. People mistakenly think that when you write a book, readers automatically buy it if it's in the bookstore. Not true! The shelf life of books is very short, and you must keep the readers and the bookstore buyers interested and aware of your books.

The most important thing I have learned is that I am marketing myself as much as my books, and when it comes to publicity, more so. People become well-known because they set themselves apart from everyone else by either being an expert, outrageous, outspoken, timely, or opportunistic. Disc jockeys, newspaper, radio and television interviewers want someone who will make their shows interesting and entertaining. All the authors are vying to be on their shows, but the authors who meet the interviewer's needs are the ones who will get on. Notice the products you use. Each has its own attribute, that specific reason or use for which the customer buys that product.

Think of the people you like to watch and identify with the most. We like them because they are willing to be open and reveal themselves. **Garth Brooks** says his popularity is due to his openness because he doesn't have the best voice or play the guitar the best.

The representative of Snapple Drinks is one of the most honest and revealing women I've seen. When she first appeared on a show, I thought the audience would snicker because this lady is about as wide as she as tall, and makes no pretense of being self-contained. But she was so honest and down-to-earth that everyone fell in love with her. In fact, she said that she had received several proposals from men seeing her on television, and she is wisely leery of them.

My store-owning days taught me that while your store is a reflection of the owner, you can't buy just what you like. You have to see things through the eyes of your customer. Most people follow the latest trends so you have to be up on things. I think this falls in the area of **willingness to change. Doug Larson**, United Feature syndicate writer says, *"In this fast-paced, modern world, it only takes a fraction of the time it used to for a luxury to become a necessity."*

One of my biggest mistakes was not learning to get rid of things when they were no longer in style. Marking down or even taking a loss is better then getting stuck with outdated merchandise. An old but true business adage is *cut your losses*, don't keep pouring good money after bad. Just as nature is in constant change, so should our lives grow and change. The one thing you can count on is that things will change! The US. Congress Office of Technology reports that change is happening faster than we can keep tabs on and threatens to shake the foundations of the most secure American business.

Sondra Healy, chairman of Turtle Wax which has the three top-selling car waxes, is known for her marketing and product creativity. Healy and her husband, parents of three children, run the company founded by her father 53 years ago. She has a B.F.A from the Goodman School of Drama and an M.A. from the National College of Education which is further proof that you do not have to major in a field to be successful. The company does $125 million.

How to Find Your Market

Women entrepreneurs should find out more about selling to the federal government because it is now a $200 billion-a-year consumer. A lot of red tape has been cut out by **The Federal Acquisition Streamlining Act of 1994.** The good news is that by the year 2000, all purchases in the $2,500 to $100,000 range will go to small businesses. Through your computer you will be able to bid on contracts with The **Federal Acquisition Network** (FACNET). Formerly, business owners seeking to sell to the government had to register with each agency. Now certification is a one-step process and suppliers can come from all over the nation. You can call the electronic Commerce Information Center at 1-800-334-3414 to find out about VANS, Value Added Networks which will break down the requests for your area.

One of the best sources to find new consumers, and experts in your area and see the latest products is find out about the conventions being held in every field. **The Directory of Conventions** (Successful Meetings, New York City) can be found at large libraries.

If you live in a large city, your newspaper publishes a list of upcoming conventions. Trade publications have a column called "upcoming events" that announce the dates.

If you can't attend the convention of your choice, you can write for a free preliminary program which describes the technical seminars. This provides the names of experts and how to contact them. Don't be afraid of contacting experts because most of them are very willing to pass along their knowledge. Successful people are aware that we are all connected and that we get back that which we give out. Each of them probably had a mentor or others who brought them information when they needed it.

Sherri Medina, only 34 years old, started a physical, occupational and speech therapy service company in 1988 and is now bringing in sales of $20 million. She had no formal business education, and depended on others for their expertise. She learned from getting ideas from several successful people.

Roy Speer and Lowell Paxson found a huge market when they figured out that people like to shop and they like to watch television and they would really like to shop while they are watching TV. This is how The Home Shopping Network, Inc. got started.

All my book signings have benefited me immensely because another author or bookstore employee has been willing to share his or her knowledge. Several people have called me seeking information about self-publishing books. Actually, I love to talk about it.

Your library has a book listing every association and when their conventions and meeting times take place.

I have found this particularly useful in contacting groups about doing motivational speaking. Being women gives us an inside track on how to market to women. **Brenda J. Lauderback** is president of US. Shoe Corporation Footwear Wholesale, a **$2.6 billion** business marketing of Bandolino, Capezio, and Easy Spirit shoes.

Marketing Strategies:

1. **Build confidence in your business.** Advertising appears to make price the customer's number one factor, but confidence, then quality, followed by service are the most important factors for customer loyalty.

2. **Keep up with the latest marketing strategies.** For instance, my books are being advertised on the Internet. Carefully investigate how to spend your marketing dollars. Women are inclined to be too trusting and therefore willing to believe the coupon salesman and others seeking your advertising money whether that form of advertising will bring you any response or not. I found that I made better choices when I was not being pressured by the salesperson. An old ploy is that you must act today. Remember, that if it doesn't feel right, it isn't right.

3. **Customers are looking for convenience.** Time and effort are such important issues, especially for women, because most have jobs and families. Many a shopping center has failed because organizers have made parking in front of the stores impossible. Busy people really resent a store wasting their time by having them wait in line.

Sydell Miller owns the nation's largest professional hair-care company, with more than $200 million in annual sales. Besides just selling hair products, Matrix markets cosmetics and skin care products. Annual sales have grown 60% since 1980. Before Sydell started Matrix, she owned a salon called Arnold's Hair Designs. The Miller's salon was one of the first to offer facials, nail care, retail products and a women's clothing boutique. The business's growth was constant. Women liked the idea of one-stop shopping. Matrix's first-year sales topped $650,000 and then reached $3 million by its third. Matrix is now located in 24 different countries and is still expanding.

4.   **You shouldn't try to go head on with your competition.** Instead, find a niche for your business. Did you watch as Wal-Mart grew into a giant? They focused on the smaller markets where K-Mart and other stores weren't located. IBM controlled the computer business, but Apple concentrated on personal computers, Sun, in workstations, and Digital in minicomputers. Or if a niche seems to be taken, find a better way to service it.

Domino's Pizza met a need by delivering to the home. You would be surprised at how many books are sold in places other than in book stores. Large corporations have shows where vendors have booths to sell their products. You can market by direct retail. Many products are sold as a tie-in with other products.

5. **Look for markets that are not already saturated by finding a new product category.** Chrysler Motors was about to go under until the company started producing the mini-van and took the risk. Top officials saw the young mother's need for a vehicle to transport the children.

6. **Be inter-connected.** A spiritual person understands the benefits of being inter-connected and so should businesses. If you meet someone in business and you would like to build on the relationship, send them a newspaper article they'll be interested in. It's good to give talks to local organizations because you are networking and getting publicity. Fusion marketing is when businesses tie-in. McDonald's constantly does it with movie characters and the travel industry ties in with transportation, motels, and entertainment.

7. **Advertise postively.** Political campaigns have seen the backlash of negative advertising and so have businesses. Consumers are blasted with enough negativism on the news, the stock market, and the latest information about the gross national product. Our country has always been creative and resourceful, and if we quit telling people what they can't do instead of what they can do, it will stay powerful. Spiritual people know that there is no limit to our information because we can access all the know- ledge from the past and capitalize on it for the future. Most CEO's will tell you that they receive divine inspiration! But you don't have to be a CEO to get the wisdom of the ages.

8. **Lighten up!** Business owners are doing their own television commercials and the ones who are successful are sincere and entertaining. People like dealing with someone they feel they know and can trust.

It has been interesting to watch the battle between the giants, AT&T and MCI. People like to root for the underdog and MCI plays their commercials to that fact.

"What are you afraid of AT&T?" is MCI's question. Both companies are appealing for customers to trust them.

9. **Don't make assumptions and judgments.** As a new store owner, I learned that you couldn't tell who had the most disposable income. Often the people who lived in the biggest houses were "house poor" and the person not trying to keep up appearances was able to buy more. Big businesses have this problem too. IBM was rocked by the arguments between Tom Watson and his son about whether to sell personal computers some years ago. The answer might look obvious in retrospect, but at the time no one knew that almost every household would have one.

10. **Expand your thinking and you will expand your market**. The Swiss had control of over 90% of the watch market at one time. Seiko came along and produced a digital watch. Timex produced a low-cost watch which took most of the market, but then Seiko took much of Timex and Bulova's business by offering 2,300 models for customers to choose from. If you limit your world by staying in the same circles and lack a sense of **awareness** of what's going on in other worlds, you'll not only live a dull, isolated life, but be unsuccessful.

Ted Koppel says, **"We are losing our ability to manage ideas, to contemplate, to think. We are becoming a nation of electronic voyeurs, whose capacity for dialogue is a fading memory, occasionally jolted into reflective life by a one-liner: "Where's the beef?" "Today is the first day of the rest of your life." "Born again." "Gag me with a spoon." "Can we talk?" Yes we can talk; but only at the level of the lowest common denominator. We are imposing on our minds the same burdens that we have inflicted on our stomachs-**

precooked ideas- designed to appeal to the largest number of people at the lowest possible price: McThought."

My next project is to publish my *Life's Instruction Books* for Women in Spanish- to also be sold here in the United States as well as Spanish speaking countries. Those who consider people from other countries as interlopers are missing out on expanding interests, knowledge, and markets.

10. **Call back and follow-up.** You may think the letter you sent advertising your company's services or products is self-explanatory, but you need to make that personal contact. A self-employed or small business owner has all the areas of his own business to attend to. She might be interested in your company but it's not the most important issue of the day. And the person who works for a larger company may not have a vested interest. Many times mail does not get to the right person and it sits on someone's desk or is thrown away.

Make that extra phone call to see whose attention your advertisement should be addressed. Most buyers need to see a product at least three times before they buy.

11. **Don't take your present customers for granted.** Repeat business is a lot easier to get than new business. Connect with your customers and ask them what they need.

12. **Focus.** Just as you have learned to respect your individuality as a person and disregarded the wasted energy of worrying about competition, your business should focus on being innovative and creative. **A**

business, like our bodies, has to be a constant recreation of itself or it dies.

Robert and Ellen Wallace, owners of Arizona Sun Products, retail, wholesale, and do direct-mail of skin-care products and gifts. They were creative when they needed 500,000 items packaged. They paid a local church group $1,000 to round up 200 kids to work, eat pizza, and listen to music. The couple took no salary for four years, but now the business does over a $1 million. Their start-up costs were $1,000.

13. **Be aware of changes.** Change is a given and people's buying habits make radical turnarounds. In a world where people are lining up to buy denim clothing that has been shot with gunshot to the big bucks women are willing to pay for the miracle bra, we never know what'll come around again or be hot on the market. **Linda Wachner,** President of Warnaco, came up with the idea of the miracle bra. Wachner also heads Authentic Fitness, which makes the Speedo, Anne Cole, Catalina, and White Stag lines. Warnaco's Miracle Bra boosted profits for this intimate-apparel and men's wear manufacturer. Sales are now at $789 million, making her the seventh top women's business owner.

Warnaco made a financially wise decision when it decided to market with the Avon Corporation. The company is also telemarketing on the STAR Network broadcasting to Asia and Middle East. Wachner's company is ranked in the Fortune 500 and has increased sales by 80% since 1986.

Another example of joint-venture marketing is Jockey International men's briefs licensing with Tommy Hilfiger men's underwear line. Jockey started making men's briefs during the mid 1930s and now has captured approximately 30% of the men's market.

Ron Socino owns Socino's Formalwear, a 25 store chain of tuxedo shops in St. Petersburg. He talked Pepsi into helping underwrite his annual prom season promotions when he gives out 10,000 tee shirts with every tuxedo rental. Pepsi supplied 12,000 tee shirts and his prom business rose 15%.

When I owned my store, I didn't want to sell at a loss so I got stuck with hundreds of rolls of cotton ribbon when moiré and wired taffeta became the choice. In spiritual terms, we say "let go" of defeating ideas, memories, or mistakes. In the retail world, this would have applied big time.

14. **Plan your buying.** "It's on the water" was a dreaded term when I owned my store because it meant that there was no set time for merchandise to arrive from overseas. You need back up sources for ordering goods. Figuring out the various price structures offered to small and large customers makes such a difference in your price points and profit margin. Small business owners have to pay more per square foot for their retail space, and then pay more for their goods because they buy smaller amounts. If your market will bear it, focusing on deep purchasing in a few areas is preferable to trying to cover vast areas.

Also, if you have an intuition that something is going to sell well, you need to order as much as you can, because hot items always sell out and are impossible to reorder.

15. **Good marketing is a perception of value and being in the mind of the customer.** Don't assume that what is selling in your area is what's going on in other areas. I

live in Atlanta, so, of course, Coca Cola is more prevalent, but Pepsi is stronger in other areas. You must focus your business so that one word comes to mind when your customer thinks of you.

16. If you feel that the market is already covered, focus on the specific market you want to capture. One of the problems with big department stores is that they try to be everything to everybody. Lots of buyers like smaller stores with narrower focuses and wider selection. The computer industry has such a periphery of products that a person can choose an area like minicomputers, super-computers, or mainframes to corner the category. Just as our universe is unlimited, so is the market place.

17. When you focus on a specific market or category of selling, make sure your marketing reflects the atmosphere and feeling of the market. I get a definite reality check when I walk into a mall store selling clothes to teenagers. The loud music, either black or overly bright colors, and the ambiance of the store lets me know that I'm out of my comfort zone.

18. Plan for enough money. Most small businesses suffer from under-funding. To make money, you have to be realistic about what equipment and materials you need to be competitive in the market place. If you skimp on the essentials, as my printer friend did when he bought a used press that was slow and required constant maintenance, then you narrow your profit margin by ineffectiveness and time-consuming labors. At times, lack of money may make you be creative about your marketing though. To cut your mailing costs, you might offer a business customer a discount if the customer includes your brochure in a mailing.

19. **Be willing to take a chance and run the risk of failure.** Most of the time, the greatest rewards come from taking the biggest chances. Your product or idea may not be bad, but it's packaged wrong, the timing or marketing is wrong; however, changes may make it successful. I talk to women who have ideas or want to start their own businesses who do nothing because they are afraid of what others will say if they fail. The spiritual woman will know that we are not accountable to anyone except ourselves and God. We are not responsible for making others happy or fulfilling their dreams. Our loved ones try to shelter us from hurts because they have been afraid to take a chance with their lives. Or they concentrate on our weaknesses rather than their strengths. When we are chance-takers and become directed, we open up to reveal the power within. When we put our full efforts and minds into our purpose, there is never any failure because we learn information from every expanding experience that increases our knowledge.

In 1983 **Karen Behnke** started Pacific-Care Wellness Co. in San Francisco to provide work-site health programs. I wouldn't recommend the way she got her money for start-up costs, using credit cards. She said if you open them all on the same day they will be approved. But I do admire that she worked for three years without a salary and it paid off because her company now has $6 million in revenues.

Risk-taker **Jim Noble** started Noble Oil Services in Sanford, North Carolina, in 1984 in a two bedroom apartment. He had 15 employees who had to be gone before the other residents got home. Each room was converted into an office or laboratory. Jim didn't take a salary for a year and a half, but now the company has $5.4 million in revenues.

20. **Be aware of the what's going on around you.** When I owned my stores, I would take time out to visit other stores for inspiration. You should not worry about your competition or try to copy them, because small business owners like becoming friends and passing on ideas. Better yet, talk to people in your similar business who live in another city. They will not feel that you are a competitor. We live in an unlimited world, and do not need to fear about limited markets if we continue to improve our service or product. Listen to what's on people's minds. Sometimes consumers buy because everyone else is buying something. There are other times when people buy products just because they are different.

When most of us were growing up, yogurt was something weird people from other countries ate. Later it became a replacement for ice cream because people thought it was not fattening. When consumers found out it too was fattening, they demanded nonfat. If you had been trying to sell nonfat yogurt a few years ago, you probably would not have been successful.

The words **stress** and **energy** exemplify our thinking in the '90's. Consumers are looking for hassle-free living. They are now willing to pay more for a quality product because they have had to replace inferior, cheaper products. People know which brands mean quality and they will be loyal to them.

When I was growing up, everything from Japan represented poor quality. The reason our perception and preference for Japanese products has changed so that we often buy Japanese over American products is because they constantly changed and raised their levels of quality control. After World War II, in 1950 , **Dr. Edward Deming** went to Japan to teach the union of scientists their quality control. Now each year companies receive the Deming Award to signify excellence.

The spiritual person knows it is important to increase the personal standards in his or her own life. When you are dedicated to high standards, you will be interested in increasing them in all of the areas of your life. You won't be happy to concentrate on one area without being concerned with all areas.

To succeed, we must set our standards high, change our belief system using our inner thinking and change our strategies. Ghandi said that we must do good in all areas of our lives. People who are happy and content with their lives and living a life of flow are more enthusiastic.

"The man who makes everything that leads to happiness depend on himself, and not upon other men, has adopted the very best plan for living happily." Plato

21. **The businesses which are doing well now are in the service industry.** We will see manufacturing that produces service products, those designed specifically for the consumer, will do well. One reason that mid-sized businesses are doing so well now is that they can react more quickly than big business.

The color Williamsburg blue was the dominate decorating color a few years ago. I watched to see how many years it would take Rubber Maid to make garbage cans, drainers, etc. that would match these kitchens, and it took a long time. If another company had produced the right color, they would have sold a lot of products.

We have coffee makers in black, white, and forest green now. This is one of the areas in which women are superior to men. We realize that other women like co-ordinated merchandise and will go to the trouble to put outfits, sheets, rooms of furniture, and whatever together. Moreover, we will pay more for the right color. This is what is called situational value.

Atlanta has a department store chain called Rich's, which was founded by a man who built his business on customer satisfaction. Rich's has a return policy that is unbeatable and therefore has great customer loyalty. Many customers will only buy from Rich's Department Store because they perceive that the quality is better there.

When it comes to electronics and technical products, consumers are also willing to pay more because they know if they get qualified assistance in buying the right product for their needs, it will save them in the long run.

Atlanta-based Home Depot became such a success because the company trained their employees to be very knowledgeable about home tools and products. It has been interesting to watch them try to market various products, many of which were bad mistakes. Once I saw dried flowers in their stores, items which are easily broken and destroyed. Very few people have the knowledge or desire to work with dried flowers. The company has the perception of having the lowest prices which saves the customer time in not having to shop around.

Our perceptions of ourselves can be based on exterior values or we can have low self-esteem and still be successful in some areas, but we will never demonstrate our creativity or find joy in our successes without high self-esteem. Our self-esteem creates specific expectations about what we think is possible for us. These expectations dominate our actions which then become our realities. What we think will happen in the future will predict more than the way we have acted in the past. Thus our realities confirm our beliefs a self-fulfilling prophesy in all the areas of our life such as work, personal, spiritual, physical, and mental.

The owners of Home Depot were men who were laid off from Handy City Stores. They were unemployed and could have decided that they were worthless, but they convinced someone with financial backing that they had a good idea. There had always been a need for all the products associated with a home, but no one had enough foresight or big enough thinking to put them in one store. They say people are more interested in working and staying around their homes, or cocooning. I think that because there are so many products to buy which make our homes more pleasant, people are enjoying fixing up their homes as a hobby, and they are staying home more.

The rising divorce rate has caused many women to be caretakers of their homes. Learned helplessness has changed to "I am woman; I can handle a chain saw." The smart business will recognize that women spend most of the money if they are married, and will make all the decisions if they are single. And since women are more detail-oriented, they make better shoppers.

I find it amusing when salesmen think they can outsmart a woman shopper. A friend interested in buying new carpet explained her exact specifications for purchasing new carpet to a female salesperson who showed her several choices that might work. The saleslady had an appointment and turned over the job to a man who was given the same specifications. He proceeded to show the customer the most expensive carpet that had none of her desired qualities. By the way, he lost the sale.

22. **Every line of products, like our various businesses has its own vocabulary.** The smart marketing person will not try to impress the buyer with extensive terminology, but will seek common grounds of understanding. I am no longer intimidated by people who speak business or a technical language that I don't understand, because I know a vocabulary in other markets which they do not understand.

Changes in the Marketplace and Employment

Women who decided to re-enter the work market after staying home a few years found that office equipment changed from the typewriter to the computer and fax machine. Today businesses are looking for people who are multilingual and highly educated. Top companies are dealing with people around the world so it will be necessary to find employees who can speak more than one language. People who work with computers every day are having trouble keeping up with the new software, CD Roms, scanners, and even terminology. Not being able to work on a computer in any job or field will limit your capabilities. Jobs in the future will be more team and project oriented. Employees will find it necessary to market their services by communicating with different people and adapt to various environments. Our world will continue to be more technical and global.

In the future we are going to see a growing number of independent contractors, consultants, and project managers. Jack Welch, GE Chairman, says, **"The change in the 90's will make the 80's look like a picnic, a walk in the park. Simply doing what worked in the 80's will be too slow."**

Employees and business owners must monitor the changes. In 1992 2 million workers worked at home telecommuting one or two days a week. The number is expected to increase to 7.5 and 15 million by the year 2,000. Part-time and contingent workers paid on a project basis can choose more flexible hours or work locations.

Women now represent 40% of the information-systems employees, but only 8% of the top positions.

They report that they like their jobs of exploring new technology and then applying it to business problems. New uses for computers and new software mean that there is new learning each day. Women have the opportunity to move into managerial positions.

If you like working with computers, you might want to be a computer-software engineer because of the high growth: 130% increase in employment. The development and design programs which software engineers develop have so many areas to still access. Women will need to demand equal payment in this field.

Every large corporation has to be willing to change and watch market trends. For example, Sears could not decide if they were a clothing store or a hardware and appliance store. As a result, consumers could nor find any depth in their product selections. K Mart Corporation did not up-date their look and their stores, and did not focus on the market they were trying to reach until a few years ago.

All three of these corporations should have relied on some spiritual laws. First, the public is more conscious of natural healing, the connection between mind, soul, and body, and that success can not be achieved with artificially induced quick fixes. Amazingly, now we are being told that synthetically produced vitamins do not produce as good results as vitamins of natural foods.

Companies which are directed by their mission purpose and spiritual leaders and employees will seek the best decisions in the areas of **a) site selection, b) employee education and happiness through job satisfaction, c) fairness in company hiring and firing, promoting, and allowing employees to make decisions and take responsibility, d) fulfilling**

customer's needs, e) and for being ecologically responsible.

Those companies that are aware of our human interconnectedness are returning to having a human answer the phone instead of having the caller get caught up in the maze of digital answering systems that say the company's time is more valuable than the customer's. How many stores have copied the WalMart greeter? Our first impression and often our last impression is formed in the first five seconds.

People are becoming more spiritual and are discovering that it is okay to love yourself and it is important to have balance in your life. Every mall now has body stores that feature all kinds of lotions and products to rub on your body that reflect our need to care and connect with our bodies through massage and touch. When you become aware of your body type and disposition you will also have an interest in Aroma Therapy. You will notice that every mall has at least one body shop, where a few years ago there were none.

Laura J. Peck started her company, selling bath and body products, from scratch. Her products are sold at major department stores and boutiques such as Saks Fifth Avenue, Neiman Marcus, and Henri Bendel. She started her business in 1989 and is now making sales over $2 million. A whole industry has started booming because of our spiritual interest in becoming balanced in the area of our senses.

Each of us has certain smells which alienate or inspire our bodies and you are already aware of those that are perfect for you. You do not have to go to a body shop to get the smells of nature.

Speaking of nature, female biologists represent 37% of employees and they are finding that upper-level jobs at pharmaceutical and bioengineering firms are opening to women. Major companies in this field are known for hiring and promoting women. They also allow for flex time, job sharing and child-care leave policies.

When the National Institues of Health lowered the acceptable level of cholesterol by 20%, millions of Americans changed their eating habits which initiated new packaging laws, reduced fat in foods, and sparked millions of dollars in sales for exercise machines. The success of your business, new idea, or invention must respond to the new trends, medical opinions, buying and living habits and economic conditions.

Lois Rust's Company, Rose Acre Farms in Seymour, Indiana, now provides liquid eggs to institutions such as schools, hospitals, and nursing homes because of the fear of salmonella in fresh eggs. She and her seven children took over the company in 1987 after a bitter divorce from her husband, David Rust. The company does $144 million dollars as the third-largest egg producer of fresh eggs. Rust, described as a cautious, shy woman, proves that a mother will do whatever to protect her children.

Have you watched the changes going on in bookstores? A few of them sell only audio books. The mega bookstores now sell music, multimedia, and computer CD's. Again because this is such a new field, women are making great strides. The membership of the National Multimedia Association is 33% women. The field has increased sales, but because it is such a new area, many companies are failing.

Liz Claiborne was a clothing designer with the Jonathan Logan Company for 16 years. She suggested changes because she felt the limited variety of patterns and sizes was insufficient to meet the changing needs of their market. She started her own company offering designs for working women and became number one in the fashion industry.

Racing Strollers is an 11-year-old company that makes three-wheeled strollers for joggers. They were the number one producers, but copies made outside of the U.S. were selling for half the price. The company had to look at how to save production costs because, while they emphasized quality, they got bogged down in the process. A consultant showed them how to cut down the steps in producing the strollers so they were able to reduce half the steps and save on production costs.

You Don't Have to Reinvent the Wheel

Many women whom I speak to say they don't have a clue about what they want to do. The fact is that there are 37,000 different jobs in the United States, so if you don't know what you want to do, you haven't investigated very thoroughly. It has been said many times, but it's still true: we spend more time planning our vacations or, with women, our marriages, than we do planning our lives.

I spent two hours the other night counseling Gayle, one of my best friends, about the latest man in her life. She had just spent two weeks taking a real estate course but hadn't made plans to take the test. When I asked her about why she had taken the course and her plans for making money, she had given it little thought. Gayle is pretty, intelligent, and talented, but she doesn't take the time to put her own needs first.

Many women have become successful buying rather than starting a new business. **Sharon Snyder** is the CEO of Cornbelt Chemical Company, a crop protection product distributor which she bought in 1976. She had worked for the company for 10 years but she added new product lines and more territory so now the business does $122 million in sales. Snyder has an A.A. from McCook Junior College and disproves the idea that you must have a four year degree to be successful.

Build on your name. Sometimes companies are able to go in other areas because of name recognition. Look at book covers. Any author who has ever had a best seller or Pulitizer Prize announces it on the covers. Brokers put together people in business transactions. They get rich by sharing in the equity of the deals so it's wise to do as many deals as possible.

Mary Robinson took the job of Irish president, which had previously been a ceremonial position, and became a highly visible, peace, and social justice leader in 1990 in a country that needs both.

Find A Need

Can you imagine a time when someone had not invented paper clips, safety pens, the telephone, post-it-notes, ball point pens, dishwashers, clothes dryers, televisions, computers? Karl Vesper's book, *New Venture Strategies,* says that the inventor of Q-tips did so because he saw his wife trying to clean their baby's ears with toothpicks and cotton. **Ann Moore** patented the Snugli baby carrier. The young Colorado mother was inspired by the carriers she had seen used in West Africa while serving the Peace Corps.

The automatic toaster was invented because **Charles Strite** was fuming at the burnt toast in the factory lunchroom where he worked. On the other hand, everything has not been invented! But just as Leonardo de Vinci was able to foresee airplanes and other great inventions, we are able to connect with God, the infinite source of all that is to be created.

Betty Nesmith found a need when, as an executive secretary, she noticed that the new electric typewriter caused more typing errors. She put together a water-based paint and a coloring agent to blend with the paper and created "white-out" for typewriters. Nesmith spent five years filling all the orders for her company, Liquid Paper Corporation, which she sold to Gillette in 1979 for $ 47.5 million.

Almost every woman in America can bake a cake, but **Sherri Paul Brown** who started Paul's Pastry Shop Inc. makes all kinds of cakes. She shipped over 5,000 cakes during Mardi Gras alone. She has 33 employees working year round making king cakes for Valentine's Day, Christmas, and birthdays. She brought in sales of $1 million in 1994.

Lane Nemeth was a day-care administrator who purchased books, toys, and games for the center. When she had her own daughter she was unable to purchase the same materials from the educational supply houses except through the center. With the suggestion and support of her father and husband, Nemth quit her job and started selling the toys. Now her business, Discovery Toys Inc., sells toys that teach spatial relations, pre-reading skills, and creative play. The company has 30,000 distributors and $93 million in sales.

Nemeth said that she had a vision about the company's mission. She decided that its purpose was to help parents realize the benefit of playing with their children. The Whole Child is a seminar that gives parents help in raising kids.

Discovery Toys now makes clothes for children so they can dress themselves. Their Body Pals is a line of personal-care products. Additionally, they are selling a line of software that helps children grow socially.

Forty years ago, **Joan Johnson** and her husband founded Johnson Products which sold black hair care products. When they divorced, she won the company in the settlement and sold it to IVAX for $67 million.

In 1987 **Mary Naylor** borrowed $2,000 from her mother to open up Capitol Concierge Inc. Naylor provides hotel style concierge services for office buildings. She services her clients' needs. Now her business is grossing $65 million and has 105 employees in 80 buildings.

Remember when people had only plastic flowers to decorate their homes? Bored with their lives, Marian, a housewife and Bill, a factory worker, began the first importing of silk flowers. **Marian Sullivan** took full charge of the business when Bill died and she began traveling around the world to find decorative items. They began the business with $13,500 and it now grosses $18 million.

Fannie Huff started an outerwear manufacturing business, now called Wyoming Woolens, in her home for $100. She knew that people needed warm clothing if they lived in areas like hers. She now has 100 employees and sales of $3.2 million. Huff had several setbacks, including personal and business bankruptcy, but she worked as a waitress to save enough money to buy a sewing machine.

Gail Frankel saw a need for children's products such as a plastic device that clips onto strollers to hold drinks, hooks for purses and bags, a car snack tray and a bubble bath dispenser. She said she wasn't really looking for success when she started her company, Kel-Gar, but now her products are sold in Toys R Us and Wal-Mart and boast sales at $1.5 million.

Chris Birchfild took $200 from her husband who was saving money to buy a cow and began an upscale baggage business in her home. She now sells tote bags, garment bags, handbags, and sporty drawstring bags to big-name companies such as Laura Ashley, L.L. Bean, and Saks Fifth Avenue. The $200 has turned into sales of $21 million.

Marla Sanders was tired of having to wait weeks to find a nanny so she decided she would open up her own agency. Her agencies are designed for working parents. Her no-nonsense approach has paid off bringing in sales of $2.4 million in 1994. She now owns the country's largest privately owned nanny agency.

Kimberly Mattson, only 33 years old, started a company selling women's underwire sports bras. She started the business in 1993 and is now bringing in sales of $1.5 million plus. She wanted to build a company where her employees would enjoy coming to work. Her office has an oceanfront view so there are no complaints from her 18 employees. She claims that her product is special because it's the only sports bra sized to fit.

Robert Horgan saw the need for a system to centralize bookings for hotels and show agents how to maximize revenues. He started Newmarket Software Systems Inc. in 1985 with the goal of automating the whole world of selling. His company now does $12 million dollars a year and is used by Sheraton, Hyatt International, Omni, Holiday Inn, and Doubletree. He has plans to service all the small chains in the U.S. Horgan risked everything when he mortgaged his home and lived on nothing for four years while his business was starting.

Your Job Should Reflect Your Purpose

> "Figure out what your most magnificent qualities are and make them indispensable to the people you want to work with. Notice that I didn't say work for." Linda Bloodworth-Thomas

No one will ever say that looking for a job is fun or easy, but doing your homework about the best procedures and tactics will make your search more directed and the results more fulfilling. When you decide to first fulfill your purpose in life, and live a life of service, then your first approach won't be to just look in the newspapers. You will ask to be divinely guided to your perfect job.

First, take time to adjust your attitude so that you are seeking the "perfect" job for using your individual talents, abilities, intuition, and wisdom. Unfortunately, only a few of us recognize that our potential for greatness is **already within us.** And that we have access through our minds to the *ultimate* "data bank," the *infinite* "creative source," and *supreme* "problem solver." Don't just look for a job to pay the bills, create your own reality by finding a job that will give you opportunities for growth, expressing your true self, and your potential.

Gettin It Done, by Andrew DuBrin Ph.D., shows a new meaning of self-discipline. DuBrin believes that the meaning of self-discipline is the ability to accomplish your goals to the fullest. Strengthening your self-discipline makes you more productive and helps you achieve better interpersonal relations.

"Great minds have purposes, others have wishes. Little minds are tamed and subdued by misfortune, but great minds rise above them." Washington Irvin.

Here's some creative job hunting tactics:

1. Approach a company with the idea of **what you can do for them.** Everyone sends out resumes, which usually have the cover letter torn off by a screening person, that helps the company screen **out** people. Instead, write a persuasive letter telling the company what you can do for them. That will certainly get their attention instead of asking about salary, benefits and overtime. Place your self in the employer's position and look through his or her eyes.

2. **Reflect your spirituality.** Removing the limitations and pain caused by the **false personality**, with all its insecurities, fears, worries, emotional dysfunction and instabilities, will reveal your true self. Employers don't want time and energies wasted with friction and jealousy among employees. Show a non-judgmental attitude by speaking and finding only good things to say about your former and present employer and associates. Show that your live in the present and are open to new and changing ideas.

This is the reason so many of us tape up a copy of, *Lord grant me the strength to accept the things that I can not change, the courage to change the things I can, and the wisdom the know the difference.* Paraphrased, this quote says, "Don't spend too much time with things you can't control, because you will be neglecting the things you can control. Probably the most important thing we can remember is that *we can not change others,* so we can should conserve our own energy and sanity by remembering we can change our attitude about what they say and do.

When I sold car phones I realized how much people focus on the negative responses of other people. A salesperson might talk to 50 people that day and encounter one really rude person. And then the salesperson would react and then preserve this person's behavior in their brain by telling everyone in the office about the negative event. They rarely spoke of the 49 nice people! **Thomas Dreier** notes, *"Talking about your grievances merely adds to those grievances. Give recognition only to what you desire."*

Thomas Moore in *Care of the Soul* says that you can read a business and get a sense of its soulfulness. During the Renaissance the Italians believed that what we physically surround ourselves with generates a kind of spirit. When you are able to spend time viewing a quiet lake, you know this is true. We've all been in homes or buildings that either soothe or disrupt us. An office filled with beautiful live plants says that we care about our world. In the same sense, the way a business treats its employees or you as an owner or employees treat others reflects your sense of spirit.

Women are especially cognizant of color and furniture choices which reflect the attitude of a business. Our recent love affair with the color mauve has cetainly been overdone. It's hard to imagine how people are able to work in bubble gum pinks and purple walls without turning green. Companies following trends have paid decorators to make choices without regard to the image they are trying to portray.

3. Put your desire for **connectedness** with others to practical use. Join a job finding group to share leads,

receive help improving resumes and interviewing skills. Networking groups are listed in the newspaper. The old saying, "it's who you know" is true and accounts for 80 percent of all jobs. When you need to have something fixed at your house, don't you like to get the recommendation of a friend who has used that person? Actually, with a recommendation, you may be able to go over the personnel department and be interviewed by someone who has the power to hire you.

4. **Use your psychic abilities.** We all have extrasensory awareness with an extra strength in either **psychic vision, hearing, intuition, or feeling.** Having spent time increasing your perceptual powers, you will be able to better connect with the interviewer and have insights into the kind of person they want to employ. Too often we feel desperate and take a job knowing it is totally wrong for us or that the company does not have a suitable mission purpose. **Companies are seeking people who can think, solve complex problems, and be creative.** Creativity is no longer just associated with being able to draw or sing. It is finding an expressive way to do anything that you do. It is important to learn to do everything that you do to your best ability. It has been said that **"learning new things won't help the person who isn't using what he already knows."**

Everyone in business has seen companies that seem invincible come tumbling down because they did not adjust to the new technological advances and business approaches. Show the company you are an innovator! Companies who used to frown on the free spirit are now looking to them for new ideas.

5. Never put your marital status, age, birth date, number of children, weight or hair color on a resume or application form. You may think the interviewer is being

friendly when he/she is asking about your family or other questions, but they are seeking information that may keep you from getting the job.

6. When applying for a job, do not state your current salary. List the one you want to make. **If your mind can perceive it and believe it, you can receive it.** Check salary surveys in your field. Know the going rate for your job. Get the employer to state a salary first so that you don't ask for a lower salary when they might have been thinking higher. If you have to name a salary, aim high so you have some negotiating room. Pay-for-performance plans or additional vacation time are additional options.

7. It is not advisable or necessary to write down references on your resume. The interviewer may see a name he/she doesn't like.

8. Remember, you were never fired from a job. You are looking for a better job or more money. You are **not** the experiences that happen to you. Before you go into the interview, recall your strengths and purpose, and the power within.

Before I do a radio or television interview, I recall a funny incident that causes me to laugh. Laughter is the greatest nerve relaxer. You can recall a favorite song, peaceful atmosphere, successful or happy feeling that will give you a calm and serene attitude. Your body is a reflection of what is going on inside, so you don't want to appear stiff, hesitant or uncertain, closed, or hidden. **LET YOUR LIGHT SHINE!**

9. Many women have been donating their time to charities and organizations in the area of fund raising which has given them needed expertise. Consider the talents and networking connections you have made doing political fund raising or charities. Now you can get paid. Strive to change the statistics which report that women earn 25%

less than their male counterparts and are in fewer top positions.

Don't downplay the knowledge and experiences you gained working in the PTA, charities, and non-profit organizations. EM Johnson, chairman of the Cancer Society Luncheon asked me to speak in Fairhope, AL. With the help of her committee, they were able to raise $12,000. EM has the organizational and motivational skills to run any organization or business she wants. Mary Thompson, who lives in Marietta, Georgia decided that her county was a mess. She raised money from the local government, started a recycling program, pushed local police to enforce the environmental laws and formed the Cherokee County Clean Commission. Mary has also raised millions of dollars for local libraries, pushing "the adopt a stream" program and heading up the jury selection committee.

10. Of course, write a thank you note to the interviewer. Even if you don't get the job, it's a good idea to call back the interviewer for the following reasons: a) you can ask for a second interview, b) the interviewer might direct you to other companies since they are in the same field, c) they might offer constructive insights about why you didn't get the job or what you can do to improve your interviewing skills. You may not have gotten the job because the interviewer realized that you are overqualified, someone in the company may have had the job almost wrapped up and the company was "just fishing" for a better applicant, or God knew that this was not the perfect job for you and is leading you to it.

11. **Women's Sourcebook**, edited by Lisa DiMona and Constance Herndon, lists the best companies for women, and the companies with mentoring programs for women.

Spiritual Management

Corporations and businesses are finding that spiritual people are better employees because of their attitudes toward life. Women make excellent managers because of their relationship experiences dealing with families. The same principles that apply to happy successful families apply to happy successful businesses.

1. **People need to feel safe and secure knowing that they will not be ridiculed, humiliated, or put down.** The verse, *"Do unto others as you would have them do unto you"* applies to all situations in our lives. Actually, the way we treat others is a reflection of our feelings about ourselves. We can show love in direct proportion to the love we have of ourselves. We feel more comfortable with people on our same level of self-esteem. Whether you are a manager or CEO, involved in a relationship or marriage, or relating to your children, it is important to raise others self esteem by seeing the best in them.

2. **Any time we give people new tasks that show we have faith in their abilities, we will see them take additional responsibilities and become excited about their lives and jobs.** My friends, Carol and Don Wise hired Carol's brother to work in their business selling valves and gauges. Jimmy worked in the warehouse and took advantage of them thinking that because he was a relative, they would not fire him. He frequently didn't show up for work or came in late more than all the other 20 employees combined! Then, the Wises explained that they would fire him, but they also put him in charge of

running the mechanics of the business. Given this responsibility, Jimmy now comes to work each day because he is necessary to the business. His self-image has changed which is reflected by the way he acts and dresses.

3. **Companies and families are learning the benefits of brainstorming.** When we invite family members and employees to express their thoughts and feelings by listening and then incorporating their ideas, we are saying we think they are worthwhile. Can you imagine the brainstorming that must go on at the Carsey-Werner Company? Marcy Carsey and husband Tom Werner are the producers of the TV sitcoms *Cybill and Roseanne*. They now have syndication rights for *The Cosby Show* and *Grace Under Fire*. Next year they will start Werner Moving Pictures, a film division.

When families start working together rather than against each other they will be more successful. We need to pay more attention to ways to talk to each other. We would never say the things we do or use the tones that we do with strangers. Why should be treat the ones we love so much worse than we would a stranger?

4. **Time spent explaining the mission purpose of the family or business is never wasted.** When the participants are informed constructively about their performance, shown new ways, and encouraged to make decisions, they begin to use good judgment. Then they take appropriate actions and begin to excel.

5. **Mothers and bosses know that we all function better when we have clear-cut rules which they expect to be followed.** But successful moms and bosses are also

willing to readjust their thinking about rules. When problems arise, they see them as opportunities for people to learn and gain empowerment by taking responsibility for their own actions. When we ask or expect people to expand, we must allow for some mistakes and not to punish them for taking a chance.

Nancy Badore, executive director of the Ford Motor Company's Executive Development Center, trains the company's top 2000 managers emphasizing quality and customer orientation. She leads with the value system that says there are no status distinctions, and we all are empowered, which eliminates power and hierarchy distinctions. Badore says that she is intuitive, which means that ideas come to her quickly, and extroverted, which means the she is stimulated by other people. When she realized the kind of things she really liked to do, such as talk, she became more effective. When she allowed herself to be who she really was, she became more effective.

Ford Motors is recognized as a reinvented corporation whose mission purpose is on the final product. Ford began a program of employee involvement that encouraged unions, plant managers, and corporate officers to begin talking and working with one another. This was a total change from the antagonistic attitudes of the past. It must have worked because the Ford Taurus was the #1 best selling car last year.

Gail Duncan-Campagne is the President and owns 61% of Jerome-Duncan Ford in Sterling Heights, Michigan. Prior to being President, she worked in the company's finance department, was parts-and-service director and then VP of Operations. The company does $118 million which makes her one of the 50 top women business owners in the U.S.

Selling as a Profession

Commission selling is one of the highest paid professions and is a good area for women because of their natural attention to detail, their ability to communicate and their insight into the thinking of other people. If you want to find a representative for your business, call other buyers because they will know who to suggest.

No matter if you are selling a product or need to represent yourself, here are some selling suggestions:

1. Personal visits are your best sales weapon.
2. Any time you make a call make sure you don't hang up without achieving your purpose, whether it's setting a meeting or confirming it.
3. You can serve two purposes at one time if you arrange to meet a prospect at a networking event. Purchasers are more in a buying mode at trade associations meetings. But don't rule out sporting events and Chamber of Commerce events.
4. Some selling positions do not require technical knowledge of a product. A new field in which women are succeeding is credit card marketing. You have probably noticed from the direct mail that you have received that credit card companies are aligning with nonprofit organizations and charities and co-branding the cards. I have received advertisements from National Public Television, my college alumni association, and a national charity because part of my profits go to them. Some cards will get you reduced rates on car rental, free airline miles or other special promotions.

Promote Yourself

"I like women who are out there doing, I don't mean in terms of the working women vs. the non-working woman, because we all know that ALL women are working, each in their own private way. I like women who are very involved with living and who haven't pulled out from life." Colleen Dewhurst

Whether you own a company, work at home, work as a salesperson, or work for another company, you are selling **yourself** in addition to the product you are selling The tools of the trade are the same.

☑ Send prospects or customers a handwritten note, perhaps one that is imprinted with your company name and logo. For instance, I just did nine book signings in Houston and I will send a thank-you note to each of the book department managers. I want them to know how much I appreciate their efforts toward making the signing a success. Get in the habit of sending a personal note to people you meet networking, socially, or to clients and customers.

☑ Get an endorsement from a friend or ask someone respected in your field. If you are trying to establish yourself with a company, you will get better results if you are recommended by someone the company respects. Books often print quotes about the book from experts on the subject.

☑ Have letters or quotes from satisfied customers. This is not a time for modesty. Because you know your purpose, you can commit your every effort to it.

☑ Send a videotape about your product, service, or yourself. This is a great marketing tool because people are curious about what's in the video. I send videos out when I am trying to get an interview on the television station.

☑ Computer graphics gives everyone a fair opportunity to make a great business presentation using their computer and laser printer. Preprinted trifolds and stationary make your materials look professionally printed. Spend time making your printing look professional since it may be the first impression a client or company gets of you. Be creative!

☑ Take the time to develop relationships. Invite your client or prospect to a meal as a powerful way to strengthen your relationship.

☑ If you decide not to work outside the home, be sure that you stay involved and aware of the changes going on in the world.

Health Issues

Alternative Medicine

Women are beginning to take responsibility for their own health. Two years ago, the National Institutes of Health created an office of alternative medicine to investigate the scientific validity of alternative practices. This year three alternative-medical journals are being published in addition to numerous books. The First International Congress and Complementary Medicine was held in Washington, in May, 1995. Many doctors and nurses believe that managed care has sacrificed attention to the whole patient.

It is shared enterprise between practitioner and patient, and encourages users to feel that they-not a doctor or an insurance company- are in charge of their own health. Self-diagnostic tests and health-care products for preventive medical purposes are becoming more available on the market. Corporations are instituting "wellness" programs because of the rise in health-care costs and because of employee "entitlement."

It has a strong spiritual component. In a survey performed by the American Holistic Medical Association, 90 percent of a group of California practitioners said that spirituality is very important to their practices. Larry Dossey, M.D. and former chief of staff at Medical City Dallas Hospital cites more than 130 studies tying prayer with recoveries in his book, *The Power of Prayer and the Practice of Medicine.*

Success Through Spirituality For Women

There is a definitive mind and body connection. One journal published a study about grieving widows and widowers which showed they had fewer white blood cells to defend their bodies against foreign invaders. Certainly, people who demonstrate a strong faith in an afterlife and have a close connection with God will remain strong while they are still on earth because they know they will be reunited with their loved ones.

Alternative medicine is holistic, encompassing the whole patient, how he or she feels physically, psychologically, spiritually, and in relation to his or her environment. Surveys show that one in three Americans have tried some form of alternative medicine and 32 medical schools teach it. Last month, Harvard Medical School offered working physicians the first continuing education course in alternative disciplines. In the 1980's researchers discovered meditation and diet can reverse severe heart disease.

Atlantan Dr. Susan Kolb does reconstructive surgery. She also does energy medicine, which is an intuitively guided technique in which a practitioner seeks to transmit healing energy to a patient. When the body is viewed as a physical representation of a surrounding energy field, pain or illness from disturbances in the field can by lessened by modulating the field, long distance, or by laying on of hands, with healing intentions or prayer. This technique is used to speed the healing of wounds and reduce post operative pain, and to identify emotional and spiritual difficulties that could lead to disease.

When using energy medicine, practitioners transmit healing energy to modulate the patient's energy field to reduce stress and speed healing. The healer places her hands on the person's body and allows nonphysical energy to pass through them into the body. The ill body uses this energy to add to its own to help heal itself. A body and spirit lacking harmony, blocked by anger, sorrow, or resentment do not grow and change. Instead, the body holds energies that disturb its balance. Researchers at Ohio State University have found that if you are under stress because of a bad marriage, separation, or divorce, your immune system will be less protective.

Doctors are no longer afraid to speak about cases where the patient has decided to recognize certain blocks and through the release of them, the body begins to heal itself. It is important to focus on feeling worthy and the ability to become healthy. Marlene Mc Kenna suffered from a malignant melanoma cancer and was told that she would die. She prayed, mediated, learned yoga, and practiced daily visualization. Her cancer was cured.

Rheumatoid arthritis is called an autoimmune disease because the immune system attacks the body's own joints. It is considered a psychosomatic ailment because it becomes worse when a person becomes stressed. Robert Ader, a psychologist has studied the effects of **psychosocial factors:** personal relationships, stress, environment, attitudes, and behaviors about health. He found that the body is able to suppress its own immune system.

When the immune system becomes overactive because an antigen, such as ragweed pollen, enters the body, allergies result. When it under-reacts or ignores an abnormal antigen, cancer may appear because the abnormal body cells are allowed to proliferate. We get infection when our body under-reacts or is unable to destroy an outside antigen. Doctors know this is how the immune system works, but they are now recognizing that it is not self-contained and is influenced by other systems in the body.

Alternative medicine is culturally specific. Many alternative systems such as traditional Chinese medicine, Indian Ayurveda, Native American healing chants are rooted in one ethnic heritage. Pain or illness stems from disturbances in the field, and can be lessened by modulating the field long-distance, or by laying on of hands with healing intentions or prayer. You should read **Spontaneous Healing,** by Andrew Weil, M.D., a professor of medicine at the University of Arizona who writes of unexplained healings. Caryle Hinshberg's book, **Remarkable Recovery,** says that the capacity for self-healing is in all of us.

You can not ignore the spirituality, the emotions and the mind, but you would be robbing yourself of all a physician can do. Hippocrates said, "I would rather know what sort of person has a disease than what sort of disease a person has." **Love, Medicine and Miracles,** by Bernie Siegel, M.D., was the first book to popularize the belief that more than medical technology is needed to treat a person.

There is a close connection between the body and the mind and between the success of a treatment and the attitude of the person receiving it. **Imagery in Healing: Shamanism and Modern Medicine,** by Jeanne Achterberg-Lawlis, Ph. D., says that our thoughts can either make us ill or heal. Socrates said 2,000 years ago, **"There is no illness of the body apart from the mind."** Our attitudes have changed in the last 20 years so that we are reversing legislation that was against healing practices.

Alternative Medicine Terminology

Acupuncture is the use of needles inserted along pathways called meridians that restore proper energy flow to the body.

Ayurveda uses herbs, diet, meditation and yoga to balance aspects of metabolism.

Chiropractics manipulate the spine to restore nerve pathways that allows the body to heal itself.

Homeopathy uses diluted doses of medications that, at full strength, cause reactions mimicking disease symptoms which triggers the body's healing response. The patient focuses his mental resources through meditation, guided imagery, or prayer. This combats the disease, boosts the immune system, and is relaxing.

Immunotherapy is treating cancer patients by giving them injections of their own immune cells after they have been charged with agents that make them grow in strength and numbers.

Psychoneuroimmunology, or PNI says that our attitudes and emotions are linked in critical ways to our bodies, mainly our brain, nervous, endocrine and immune systems. Numerous brain chemicals that are released have been proven to affect the immune system. Evidence shows that certain psychological and spiritual states can change the healing of a disease.

Traditional **Chinese medicine** uses herbs, acupuncture, massage, and meditative exercise to restore energy flow and harmony with nature. One study by the State University of New York showed that even your saliva contains more germ fighters when you are in a good mood.

A **massage** manipulates muscles and connective tissues which reduces pain, improves strength, and relieves stress.

If you are a female over 12 you are aware that women's attitudes about sex are different than men's. A plethora of books abound discussing how our views differ. Some important concerns I have about sex are that a woman should not let a man take away her energy if it is not a mutually loving and fulfilling relationship.

The book, **Sexual Healing: Using the Power of an Intimate, Loving Relationship to Heal Your Body and Soul,** by Paul Pearsall, suggests that sex should be reflective, considerate and contemplative rather than the "don't think about it, just do it" approach prevalent today. Pearsall believes that if you want to be healthier, have an intimate, loving relationship. He should know what he is talking about. After hearing the words, "I think we've lost him," during cancer surgery, Pearsall said, "My wife brought me back from death's door and reconnected me with life." He suggests that the couple are joint healers and that intimate sex affects the health of both partners.

If you are wondering why health issues are being written in a book on women's success, I'm not surprised. My last stay at a hospital, until recently, was 24 years ago when # 1 only son was born. So you can see that I've had a healthy life and why I have not directed my attention to health issues. After all, there's all those great emotional issues!

Rhonda, a friend with psychic abilities told me I would be doing psychic healing one day. During a book signing in Mobile, I found myself really connecting with a lady. I could feel the energy going between us, and there in the middle aisle of a large bookstore, she asked if we could pray together. I took special notice when she prayed to the Holy Spirit that I might do special healing! Maybe the beginning of my work in healing is to write this chapter. After all, we can not become successful spiritually or financially if we do not feel well.

The following books would be good to read if you are interested in women's health issues.

Unequal Treatment: What You don't Know About How Women are Mistreated by the Medical Community, Eileen Nechas and Denise Foley. Both authors wrote for Rodale's *Women's Encyclopedia of Health and Emotional Healing* and discovered that no research had been done in several areas of women's ailments.

Outrageous Practices: How Medicine Mistreats Women, Leslie Laurence and Beth Weinhouse. The authors note that women are underrepresented as medical researchers and as subjects in medical tests. Leslie Laurence writes a syndicated column called "Her Health" and notes that women's complaints are seen as 'emotional' and often treated by tranquilizers.

A New Prescription for Women's Health, Bernadine Healy, MD., former National Institutes of Health director. After she took office, Dr. Healy began the 14-year Women's Health Initiative, a $625-million effort to study the prevention, causes and cures of diseases that affect women. She believes that women need to **take control of their health.** She has a vision of the Women's Health Initiative closing the gender gap.

INDEX

INDEX

INDEX

INDEX

INDEX

Other Books by BARBARA GRAY

Come Grow With Me

A non-dated calendar which offers growth directions in the areas of goals- spiritual, financial, physical, and mental-fulfilling a purpose in life, affirmations, and becoming proactive. By directing their thoughts inward, women are activating their creative and intuitive thinking and thus empowering their lives. This book gives you a place to plan the changes you want and need to make in your life. Plan an unlimited life, grow and develop to your fullest potential. $9.95 ISBN 0-9637784-3-9

Life's Instruction Books For Women

Short instructions on daily living, inner thinking, motivational thoughts, life as a single woman and relating to men are offered in a humorous, yet knowledgeable and insightful manner. Barbara Gray states that she finally awoke from her life-long state of sleep when her son said, *"Don't you get tired of being dumped on?"* $5.95 0-9637784-0-4

Life's Instruction Book For Women, Volume II

Short Instructions for daily living, relationships, steps for success, discovering your inner self, self worth, relating to men are stated as pertinent advice for women seeking to grow spiritually, emotionally and independently. *"Success After Divorce"* offers advice on changing the reader's thinking about a traumatic negative situation into a learning opportunity. The book contains some poems about the changing attitudes of women. $5.95 0-9637784-1-2

Life's Instruction Book, On Love, For Women   Volume III

Short instructions on enjoying solitude, meditations, learning to love yourself, and learning to love unconditionally are given as the reader is guided to fulfill her purpose in life. The reader is encouraged to grow by finding that purpose which she can fulfill better than any other person. Life is all about love and service! $5.95   0-9637784-2-0

Neglect Your Soul And Forfeit Your Happiness

Barbara Gray

Study as if you are going to
live forever;
live as if you are going to die
tomorrow.

Marion Mitchell